Items should be returned on or before the last date shown below. Items not already requested by othe borrowers may be renewed in person, in writing or telephone. To renew, please quote the number on barcode label. To renew online a PIN is required. This can be requested at your local library.
Renew online @ **www.dublincitypubliclibraries.ie**
Fines charged for overdue items will include postage incurred in recovery. Damage to or loss of items will be charged to the borrower.

THE POWER
OF THE HEART

THE POWER OF
THE HEART

Finding Your
True Purpose in Life

Baptist de Pape

SIMON &
SCHUSTER

London • New York • Toronto • Sydney • New Delhi

SIMON &
SCHUSTER

First published in Great Britain by Simon & Schuster UK Ltd, 2014
A CBS company

Copyright © 2014 by TWOTH B.V.

This book is copyright under the Berne Convention.
No reproduction without permission.

THE POWER OF THE HEART is a trademark of TWOTH B.V. All rights reserved.

The right of TWOTH B.V. to be identified as the author of this work has been asserted
in accordance with sections 77 and 78 of the Copyright, Designs and Patents Act, 1988.

1 3 5 7 9 10 8 6 4 2

Simon & Schuster UK Ltd
1st Floor
222 Gray's Inn Road
London WC1X 8HB

www.simonandschuster.co.uk

Simon & Schuster Australia,
Sydney

Simon & Schuster India,
New Delhi

A CIP catalogue record for this book is available from the British Library

ISBN: 978-1-47113-816-4
Ebook: 978-1-47113-817-1

Interior design Simon Greiner
Jacket design by Simon Greiner
Jacket art by Simon Greiner

The author and publishers have made all reasonable efforts
to contact copyright-holders for permission, and apologise
for any omissions or errors in the form of credits given.
Corrections may be made to future printings.

Printed in Italy by L.E.G.O SpA

Contents

Preface: My Own Path   1

PART I: PATHS TO THE HEART

1. Your Inner Power   9

2. Heart and Soul   15
   The Language of the Heart   17
   Contemplation: Hearing Your Heart's Voice   21

3. Opening to the Heart's Wisdom   23
   Contemplation: Walking in Silence   31

4. The Heart's Intelligence   33
   Contemplation: Sit and Listen   42

5. Coherence: Living in the Now   45
   The Inner-ease Exercise or Love Response   47
   Contemplation: Present Awareness   56

PART 2: THE INNER POWERS

6. The Power of Gratitude 59
   Contemplation: Three Blessings 64

7. Becoming a Person of the Heart 67
   Contemplation: A Sense of Soul on Earth 76

8. Creating Authentic Power 79
   Contemplation: Calm by Looking Deeply 91

9. The Powers of Intention and Intuition 93
   Your Intuition's Language 99
   Contemplation: Following Your Intuition 107

10. Synchronicity: The Hidden Order Behind Everything 109
    Tapping into Synchronicity 116
    Contemplation: Everything That Happens Is a Lesson 124

PART 3: HEART IN THE WORLD

11. Money and Career 127
    An Economy of the Heart 135
    Contemplation: Your Calling 141

12. The Heart of Health 143
    Contemplation: Heart of Love 153

13. Love and Relationships 155
    Spiritual Partnership 168
    Creating Love 171
    Contemplation: Loving-kindness or Compassion Practice 174

CONTENTS

14. Resilience, Fear, and Setbacks   177
    The Heart Carries You Through Fear   186
    Contemplation: Living Fearlessly   192

15. Forgiveness   195
    Contemplation: To Make Right   205

16. A Civilization with Heart   207

The Co-creators: Biographies   221

Acknowledgments   231

Photo Credits   232

Preface:
My Own Path

To realize one's destiny is a person's only obligation.

—PAULO COELHO, *THE ALCHEMIST*

I had just graduated from law school and received a lucrative offer and employment contract from one of the world's most prestigious law firms. I was only a signature away from a glorious career—and yet I decided not to sign.

I had begun thinking: What did I really want from life? What was my goal? I'd spent months looking for a job that suited me, but the prospect of joining a prestigious law firm and traveling the globe in order to advise multinational corporations on their transactions no longer seemed right for me—even though I had worked hard for that

Baptist de Pape (*opposite*)

law degree and opportunity. I felt I'd lost my way and I was worried about my future. What was I going to do? As I worried more and more, I felt that my world was slowly falling apart.

Very late one night, I found myself staring into the darkness of my bedroom, my mind churning with anxiety. Unable to sleep, I decided to get up and watch some YouTube videos on my laptop. I clicked on to a Web class with Oprah Winfrey and Eckhart Tolle called *A New Earth: Awakening to Your Life's Purpose.* Immediately, Oprah caught my attention when she said, "I don't think anything is more important than awakening to what your life's purpose is."

That made me wonder, *Was this what I was going through? Was I trying to wake up to my life's purpose?* The moment I had that thought, I felt a powerful impulse from my heart—one that I'd never felt before. It was as if my heart itself were responding to my inner questions and wanted me to listen up, right now.

When I moved my attention from that astonishing feeling back to the Web class, Tolle was saying, "It's fine to ask yourself what you want from life, but a far more important question is, What does life want from *you*? What does life have in store for you?" To find out, Tolle said, it's important to allow moments of silence into your life, because silence can let you escape the mental noise that we call "thinking." Habitual thoughts and worries can drown out other messages that life sends you—the quiet signals that can guide you to find your purpose.

That sounded like what I was going through—I was so flooded with worries that I couldn't figure out what I should do.

Looking back now on that night, I believe I was guided to that class. Oprah's and Tolle's observations completely changed my consciousness—and my life.

The next morning I decided to follow Tolle's advice and seek out silence. I went for a long walk in the woods in the pouring rain. As I tuned in to the quiet around me, I felt an intense, unprecedented sense of calm envelop me. This calmness was not just around me, it was also inside me. For the first time in my life, I was freed from the thoughts and worries that had been holding me hostage. I felt that I could ask what I should do with my life and open myself to accepting whatever answer presented itself, whether or not it fit in with my old ideas about my career and future. I realized that I'd been afraid to let myself accept that I didn't want to become a lawyer after all the work and time I'd put into it. I also didn't want to disappoint my parents, who had been proud of my academic success and career choice.

I stood still, enjoying the sense of inner peace I had found, the freedom from expectations. I silently asked, *What does life want from me?* Immediately, I felt another powerful impulse from my heart, one that was even stronger than that of the night before. It was almost painful, as if it *had* to be intense in order to make me pay attention—so that I would "get" the answer it was giving me. It felt as if my heart had actually broken open. The wave of emotion was so strong that I burst into tears.

Suddenly, I saw my purpose in life. It was crystal clear to me: I had to explore this power of the heart, this energy that had taken hold of me. I had to seek out the leading spiritual thinkers and writers and teachers of today and ask them for their insights about the heart. And I had to record their wisdom for all time. I had to make a film about the heart.

Now, obviously, my mind would never have given me this directive, because I had no background in filmmaking. And yet I never once doubted that this was going to be my task. I had awakened to my life's purpose. The feeling was so overwhelming that it left me with no choice but to actually pursue that calling: I would look at life through the power of the heart and I would make a film about it.

I went home, packed my suitcase, and mobilized a camera crew. Nothing was going to stop me from doing what life wanted from me.

The purpose of life is a life of purpose.
—GEORGE BERNARD SHAW

Over the next two years, I traveled around the world and was fortunate to meet and talk with eighteen influential spiritual leaders, scien-

tists, and thinkers from many diverse cultures and backgrounds: Isabel
Allende, Maya Angelou, Michael Beckwith, Deepak Chopra, Paulo
Coelho, Joe Dispenza, Linda Francis, Jane Goodall, John Gray, Rollin
McCraty, Howard Martin, Ruediger Schache, Marci Shimoff, Dean
Shrock, Eckhart Tolle, Neale Donald Walsch, Marianne Williamson,
and Gary Zukav. Through their inspiring, remarkable stories about
the heart's influence on their lives, these teachers made unique con-
tributions to my own vision for the movie—and to my life's path—so
I consider them to be Co-creators of the movie and this book. (Their
biographies can be found in the back of this book.)

The Co-creators allowed me the privilege of interviewing them in
front of the camera, and together we created a sensational portrait of
the heart. They provided impressive, and sometimes poignant, confirmation of my own conviction that the heart is more than just an organ
pumping blood around the body: without a doubt the heart is an inexhaustible source of love, insight, and intelligence that far surpasses
that of the mind.

The Co-creators taught me many important lessons about the
power of the heart, lessons that we share in the movie and that I also
want to share with you in this book. It turns out that there are many
powers of the heart—among them intuition, intention, gratitude, forgiveness, resilience, and, of course, love. Connecting with these powers
can bring about an astonishing transformation in your views of money,

5

health, and relationships and enable you to discover hidden talents and strengths that will help you create your best life. Because I can relay in this book more of the Co-creators' messages than I could show you in the movie, I'm also able to provide more of their suggestions for the many ways in which you can develop these powers. So, to help you on your path, each chapter contains Contemplations with which you can discover your heart's distinctive voice and wisdom.

Out of this incredible convocation of inspiring thinkers comes this treasury of spiritual and practical guidance. I hope that, with the help of the movie and this book, you will discover your own life's purpose, which is even now buried inside you like a hidden treasure. It is time to open to that treasure. It is time to discover the power of the heart.

Here is my secret. It is very simple: one sees clearly only with the heart.
What is essential is invisible to the eye.
—ANTOINE DE SAINT-EXUPÉRY

PART 1
Paths to the Heart

*Let yourself be silently drawn by the strange pull of
what you really love. It will not lead you astray.*

—RUMI

1. Your Inner Power

Many great teachers of the world's spiritual traditions describe the heart as the source of true power.

The way is not in the sky. The way is in the heart.

—BUDDHA

Whatever thy hand finds to do, do it with all thy heart.

—JESUS

Abide at the center of your being, for the more you leave it, the less you learn. Search your heart—the way to do is to be.

—LAO TZU

Today, modern science has evidence that the heart has a power that goes beyond its biological function.

ROLLIN McCRATY

Almost every spiritual tradition and all of the major world religions talk about the heart being the access point to the soul, to the human spirit, to wisdom, to intuition, these types of things. And the research is really starting to show that they've been right all along. The heart's activity responds and changes before the brain does. The heart sends measurable signals to the brain, which then responds.

 ## HOWARD MARTIN

New science has given my brain permission to believe in the intelligence of the heart. A large body of research shows that the physical heart is an information-processing center and not just a slavish blood pump. When heart/brain/body communication is optimal, it is associated with feeling emotions long associated with "heart" such as care, appreciation, compassion, love, etc. People intuitively know that heart and the qualities of the heart are real. The new science on the role of the physical heart satisfies our minds in a way that allows us to more fully believe in what we intuitively sense. It points toward an intelligence associated with the heart.

How can we connect with this intelligence and power? How can we use it to find out more about who we are and what we should be doing? Buddha said, "Your work is to discover your world and then with all your heart give yourself to it." This is what the Co-creators will help us do—discover ourselves, our center, and our purpose.

 ## MAYA ANGELOU

I believe that the heart is the most forceful, impactful element in our lives. I believe that the heart helps us to understand who we are, where we are, and how we are.

In order to connect with your heart, the first step is to recognize that it is the very essence of you.

 ## ECKHART TOLLE

The power of the heart is to be connected with who you are at the deepest level. The power of the heart is the power of life itself, the power of the very intelligence that pervades and underlies the entire universe. It is a power that lies at the very heart of the universe. So to live in connectedness with that, then you are in touch with the power of the heart.

 ## NEALE DONALD WALSCH

When the heart is cracked open, we access the most profound human secret of life and that is the secret of your true identity.

Through your heart, you find your way in the world.

PAULO COELHO

You will never, ever reach your full potential if you don't open your heart.

Through your heart, you connect with a higher form of knowing.

GARY ZUKAV

The higher order of logic and understanding originates in your heart. It is experienced in your heart. It is lived in your heart.

Through your heart, you find inspiration.

ISABEL ALLENDE

For me inspiration is essential. Creativity is essential and I can only find it through the heart.

And through the heart, you find insight. In fact, the heart gives you the insights you *need*, as well as ones that you may not expect—insights that allow you to find your way.

DEEPAK CHOPRA

Your heart knows all the answers, so put your attention there and reflect. That's the first thing you can do.

Your heart creates love and it connects you with others—with the people you love and with people you are meant to know. The heart also connects you with all other life in the world.

 ## JANE GOODALL

We think of the heart in the poetic sense, the seat of love and compassion and it's this heart that is so terribly important.

 ## MARIANNE WILLIAMSON

The truth of who we are is the truth of the heart, the truth of who we are is the love that lies beyond the body.

And your heart connects you with all of creation, the universe—with God.

 ## MICHAEL BECKWITH

Dr. Martin Luther King Jr. simply called it "The love of God operating in the human heart."

Let's explore with the Co-creators the many meanings of the heart and how we can connect with its amazing powers.

2. Heart and Soul

Remember that wherever your heart is,
there you will find your treasure.
—PAULO COELHO, *THE ALCHEMIST*

Paulo Coelho was one of the authors and teachers highest on my wish list to interview for my movie about the heart and for this book, partly because the power of the heart is the central theme in his popular novel *The Alchemist*. The main character, Santiago, travels to Egypt in search of a hidden treasure only to find out that the real treasure lies within him.

I met Coelho in his office at his apartment in Geneva—to me the holiest of holy sites, where he had written so many beautiful books. Coelho's office has a calm, serene atmosphere with family photographs and modern art on the walls. The screen of his computer showed a manuscript in progress, which made me feel like a Beatles fan between jam sessions at Abbey Road Studios, seeing a Gibson SG 1964 that John Lennon had just played.

I explained my mission and told Coelho about my study of law, how I had dreaded going against my parents' expectations, and how I'd awakened to the heart's power. We immediately resonated with each other and Coelho told me that his own heart awareness had compelled him to write. As a teenager, Coelho had known he wanted to become a writer, but his parents objected to that career choice. They also considered him unhealthily introverted and obstinate, and actually had him committed to a mental hospital when he was seventeen. At age twenty, Coelho went to law school, at his parents' request, but dropped out to travel around the world. Later he became a songwriter and a journalist.

 ## PAULO COELHO

From the moment that I realized that I wanted to be a writer, I said, "It may take ten days, ten years, or twenty years, but I am going to write." I started by writing songs; I started writing articles for newspapers. I had no choice but to follow the thing that I wanted to do.

You will never be able to escape from your heart.
So it's better to listen to what it has to say.

—PAULO COELHO, *THE ALCHEMIST*

During a walk along the ancient pilgrims' path to Santiago de Compostela in northwest Spain, Coelho had an awakening that led him to write his first book.

Coelho's story moved me to tears. He had lived and embodied the power of the heart. His story shows that sometimes you need to be terribly brave to follow your inner voice and passion when no one but you can hear or comprehend it. But your courage will be rewarded. The road from head to heart may not be short or easy, but it will lead you to your destiny.

Nothing is really a cliché when you really, really do it from the heart. And if you really feel it, and it's real, and you know people who have felt it, there is nothing clichéd about it. It will bring you to your knees. It will make you cry. And that's my job: to tell those stories in ways that surprise us and remind us of the opera that we're living with every mistake and every new chance.

—DAVID O. RUSSELL, FILM DIRECTOR

The Language of the Heart

The heart is so much more than a vital organ. Your heart is the center of your feelings. As Proverbs says, "As a man thinketh in his heart, so is he." When you express your deepest emotions, you instinctively put your hand to your heart. And when you indicate yourself in conversation, you point not to your head but to your heart.

Our language is full of expressions that refer to the heart as the seat of our feelings. We describe someone who is affectionate as "openhearted" or "warmhearted" and someone who is cold and insensitive as "heartless." Someone is near to your heart when you care a great deal about him. You give someone heart when you encourage her. You lose your heart when you fall in love. But the most captivating phrase of all to me is "to follow your heart"—to do what you love doing most.

Trust yourself. Then you will know how to live.

—GOETHE

The language of the heart is feelings. When you follow your heart, you listen not to your head, but to what you feel is right. The voice of your soul also speaks through your heart, which, like a compass, points you in the right direction. The seat of your soul—your spiritual essence—is within your heart.

 HOWARD MARTIN

Many thousands of years ago, people in various cultures all around the world saw the heart as the center of intelligence within the human system. The earliest writings I've ever seen about it go back 4,500 years ago to ancient Chinese medicine. This notion of an intelligent heart persisted throughout history.

Besides being an emotional center, the heart was long believed to hold an intelligence and have the ability to make decisions. In traditional Chinese medicine, the heart is the seat of connection between mind and body. The Chinese characters for "thinking," "thought," and "love" all include the character for "heart." In yogic traditions, the heart is literally and figuratively our internal guide. In Japanese, two different words describe the heart: *shinzu* for the physical organ and *kokoro* for the "mind of the heart."

A loving heart is the beginning of all knowledge.

—THOMAS CARLYLE

Over time, however, this age-old knowledge about the heart and respect for it became neglected.

 DEEPAK CHOPRA

It's an old Indian story that God wanted to hide the truth and said, "I want to make it interesting for people and the one place I want to put it in is their hearts, because they look everywhere else, only to discover later that the truth is in their hearts."

Many people spend their whole lives searching for fulfillment and happiness, often expecting to find it in the purchase of a beautiful house, a luxury car, or other material possessions. But when their satisfaction with these wears off, they look for other things to fill the emptiness: they change jobs, go on expensive vacations, or find a new life partner. Yet, as Santiago in *The Alchemist* discovers, the greatest treasure, your true source of happiness and fulfillment, is inside you, within your heart.

Everything in the universe is within you. Ask all from yourself.

—RUMI

MARCI SHIMOFF

Every spiritual tradition throughout history has spoken about the heart as being the seat of the soul, the diamond in the heart, the lotus in the heart, the temple in the heart. Every tradition speaks about the heart as being the essence of who we really are.

When you lose touch with your heart, you lose touch with your true self. You may feel unmoored and aimless; the world around you seems colorless, dull, and bleak. You cannot remember where you are going with your life. But as soon as you reconnect with your heart, everything begins to improve. You are never truly lost when you know your heart.

 ## DEEPAK CHOPRA

The way to connect with your soul, with your spirit, is just to bring your awareness to your heart. Bring your conscious awareness to your heart.

And the best way to connect with your heart, as Tolle, Chopra, and the other Co-creators recommend, is through silence.

Silence is the great teacher and to learn its lessons you must pay attention to it. There is no substitute for the creative inspiration, knowledge, and stability that come from knowing how to contact your core of inner silence.

—DEEPAK CHOPRA

CONTEMPLATION

Hearing Your Heart's Voice

To connect with your heart, allow yourself to find a quiet place. Sit and silence your thoughts. Let your mind go blank. Just push gently to the side any thoughts that are worrying you. Breathe into the quiet of your mind, into the space you've opened there. Listen to your feelings without words. You may hear a gentle, calming voice—not with your ears, but with your feelings. It is the voice of your heart, letting you know that all will be well.

As you listen to the inner voice of your heart, you become more attuned to your own life. You regain your sense of direction. You develop a renewed sense of who you are. You know what you want to do and why.

> *All shall be well, and all shall be well, and all manner of thing shall be well.*
>
> —JULIAN OF NORWICH

3. Opening to the Heart's Wisdom

> *Don't let the noise of others' opinions drown out your own inner voice. And most important, have the courage to follow your heart and intuition.*
>
> —STEVE JOBS

Even when we look at the heart as a physical organ, as well as a source of spiritual power, it is a marvel.

 HOWARD MARTIN

Today, science does not know for sure what makes the heart start beating. We have this amazing part of our physiology that marks the beginning of life and yet somehow, some way, science today cannot tell us exactly why it begins to beat.

Our very first heartbeat begins spontaneously. The beating starts the moment that specialized heart cells form and multiply in the fetus. The cells beat even before the whole heart has formed. And they beat in unison. No perceptible external or internal stimulus starts them beating. Beating is intrinsic to the nature of heart cells.

 ## NEALE DONALD WALSCH

The heart starts beating when God says, "Hello, I'm here." This is the beginning of life and I can prove it to you. Listen to your heart. The beat of your heart is the energy of life itself. It came from outside of your body, but it animates your body, and gives you the gift of who you are. What greater gift is there? How can we ignore that, how can we pay the most attention rather than the least attention to that?

The heart is propelled by an invisible energy—the energy of the universe, a force that permeates all matter and binds everything and everyone together. Nothing in the universe is more powerful, nothing holds more potential than that energy. It is called *chi* in Taoism, *ruah* in Hebrew culture, *prana* in the Hindu religion, and vital energy in Western philosophy. That energy originates outside the body and that energy gets your heartbeat going. It kick-starts all vital functions.

ISABEL ALLENDE

Once I heard a surgeon who was talking about heart transplants. And he was saying that he placed the organ, the transplant, in the new body where he's going to give life, and the heart is dead but not dead. And then the surgeon touches the heart, very softly, and it starts to move, and it starts to bring life to that body. And I thought, that in a way is a metaphor for how the heart is. You touch it, and when you touch it, you know where life is.

 ## MARCI SHIMOFF

The heart is where all the action happens. And the key to living a most fulfilling, rich, successful life is to keep the heart open. An open heart allows us to look at life in such a different way.

Opening to your heart means living a passionate life full of meaning and purpose. It means doing those things you feel you have to do, living the life you were born to live. In living with an open heart you align yourself with values of tolerance, harmony, cooperation, and respect for others.

 ## HOWARD MARTIN

The wisdom of the heart is really, said another way, the connection to your Authentic Power, to that source of realness and

Marci Shimoff *(opposite)*

genuineness that you have inside. It's from that place that we manifest things. That's where we get the job done, that's where we're able to move beyond our challenges and our limitations and our doubts and our fears and do the things that we really know we should do inside. That is the power of the heart in action, in its most useful way.

 GARY ZUKAV

What is the wisdom of the heart? The part of you that is the healthiest, the most grounded, the most constructive, the most wholesome contributor to Life with a capital L.

Because your heart is the essence of who you really are, it knows where you need to go and why you are on this Earth. Sometimes only the heart can let you know what you should do. Your brain has only a limited view of your circumstances, but your heart can assess every situation from a higher perspective.

When the heart speaks, the mind finds it indecent to object.

—MILAN KUNDERA

Have you ever been unable to resolve a problem, gone out for a walk to clear your head, and discovered the perfect solution? That is actually the power of the heart, opening you to the energy and inspiration around you. The moment you choose to listen to and open your heart, you tap into this powerful source of wisdom.

GARY ZUKAV

The wisdom of the heart will see the power and the beauty and the opportunity of every moment that you live and cherish each one.

Every new day gives you a new chance to open your heart. Once you do, you notice the goodness of people and things you had previously taken for granted. You become able to put disappointments into perspective; you're more receptive to the great opportunities that present themselves to you on a regular basis.

By opening your heart, you become aware of the deeper dimension of your own existence. You understand who you really are and why you are here.

 ECKHART TOLLE

The heart points to the most essential dimension within you, and not to be connected with that, and to live your life as if that dimension didn't exist, is really missing the very purpose of your life on earth, no matter what you achieve outwardly.

 DEEPAK CHOPRA

In all wisdom traditions, the real home of the spirit is non-local, which is beyond space and time. But it expresses itself locally in space-time and, yes, in most spiritual traditions the heart

is the entry point of the transcendent spirit into the world of space-time and locality.

NEALE DONALD WALSCH

The secret of the human heart is that it contains not only your identity, but God's, wrapped up in one.

MAYA ANGELOU

God speaks in the heart, from the heart. God speaks from the heart.

GARY ZUKAV

Divine intelligence is in the heart. You will not find your soul in the intellect.

Through the voice of your heart you gain access to a divine dimension, one that has been inside of you from day one. In your heart, that divine dimension and your most authentic self are one.

Blessed are the pure in heart, for they shall see God.

—JESUS

CONTEMPLATION

Walking in Silence

Every breath, every step can be filled with peace, joy, and serenity.
We need only to be awake, alive in the present moment.

—THICH NHAT HANH

Walking mindfully is a tradition in many cultures. Your brain can't dwell on worries and problems when your body is physically active. Take a walk—around your home or in a park, wherever you are comfortable walking—to quiet your mind and allow yourself to hear the voice of your heart.

Walk at a comfortable pace and be attentive to each step. With each step, you arrive here and now. You are in the present moment. Be aware of the way each foot touches the ground. Feel each point of contact, heel and toe. Stay aware of each step, and now bring your attention to your breathing. Now, with each step you take, when you breathe in, say to yourself, "In." As you breathe out, with each step you take, say to yourself, "Out." With each step and breath, as your mind becomes quieter, you open space for your heart to communicate to you.

Once you are quiet in your mind and body, bring your attention to your heart. Walk with awareness of your heart, in companionship with your heart. If you feel ready, ask your heart, *What do you want me to know?*

4. The Heart's Intelligence

The best and most beautiful things in the world cannot be seen or even touched—they must be felt with the heart.

—HELEN KELLER

Without even realizing it, we pay more attention to our minds and thoughts in day-to-day life than we do to our hearts and inner guidance. We're often locked inside our heads, having programmed ourselves to rein in our emotions and dismiss any inklings or intuition as inappropriate, scary, or strange. More often than not, when faced with an important decision, we weigh the pros and cons and decide that the rational choice is the best one.

A good heart is better than all the heads in the world.

—ROBERT BULWER-LYTTON

But how often have you thought, after making a rational decision—whether or not it worked out—*If only I'd listened to my heart*? Have you ever found at least one reason not to do what your heart told you to do for fear of someone else's reaction? Or come up with excuses not to do what deep down in your heart you want to do most? When we ignore the heart's messages, we bury our dreams and extinguish our inner fire.

 PAULO COELHO

I know a lot of people who are "dead." But they walk, they talk, they watch television. They work hard sometimes, but somehow this spark of divine energy is lost. It's not that it is lost forever. This child that you have in your soul can always say hello again and provoke this spark to manifest itself. But these people renounce the fact that they have dreams. They lose contact with the dream. A person who is disconnected from his or her heart is not living.

When you are completely out of touch with your heart, you feel uncomfortable, as if you are living on the surface, missing out on something. Whenever you are disillusioned or frustrated, ask your heart to connect you to your deepest emotions—they are the spark of divine energy that is so vital to living with purpose.

Paulo Coelho *(opposite)*

MICHAEL BECKWITH

There's an intelligence within the heart that is far bigger than our figuring out the mind.

Even though you may unconsciously follow your heart's promptings, you may not generally be aware of them. To become conscious of your heart's intelligence, simply open to your heart and listen for its inner voice.

PAULO COELHO

Don't lose hope. God finds three, four ways to kick your head and say, "Come on! Don't forget your purpose in life!" Give a chance to your dream. You are not going to regret it. I am not saying that you're not going to suffer. I am not saying that you are not going to be defeated. I'm saying you're not going to regret.

Your heart communicates to you the meaning *in* your life and *of* your life. It connects you to a greater source of knowing, to which you cannot gain access with your mind. Philosopher Blaise Pascal could not have put it better when he said, "The heart has its reasons that reason doesn't know."

Steve Jobs, cofounder and CEO of Apple, considered the heart to be the source of inspiration and fulfillment. He ascribed his achievements directly to the power of the heart: "The only way to be truly satisfied is to do what you believe is great work. And the only way to do great work is to love what you do. If you haven't found it yet, keep looking and don't settle. As with all matters of the heart, you'll know when you find it. And like with any great relationship, it just gets better and better as the years roll on. So keep looking. Don't settle."

Through your heart, you understand your greatest desire and passion, and through the heart you find the spontaneity and creativity to break through the everyday restrictions on your life and imagination—to live fully engaged. When you open to your heart, your entire world changes—it opens up around you. You see yourself as part of a friendly universe, one that is full of possibility, one that is generating and regenerating a positive energy.

 DEEPAK CHOPRA

Getting in touch with your heart is like plugging into that universal consciousness or spirit. Your heart is a little computer that plugs into the cosmic computer where everything is inseparably one.

Your heart allows you to link up to an enormous server: the universe. That server is omnipresent, even when your own connection has a glitch. When you are logged on to the energy of the universe, you gain access to the bigger picture, the interconnectedness of your life with the lives of others. Your heart knows what will make you happy.

NEALE DONALD WALSCH

If I could offer a piece of advice to all people, and especially to young people, it would be this: Use your heart. Forget your mind. Your mind will just simply wrap you up in your story, in your imagination, in your idea, usually your worst idea about things. But your heart knows the truth. Listen to your heart, and you can't go wrong. You won't.

Your heart sees your life as if it is following the course of a river—from the source down to the sea—whereas your mind cannot look beyond the next bend. Your mind is busy with a thicket of immediate concerns and short-term goals that can block your view of your larger purpose. Your mind keeps you rowing along, stroke after stroke, your back to where you're heading, so that you see where you've been only after you've already gone past. So, when you hit a snag or need to change course, you get frustrated.

But when you open to your heart, you discover that your heart knew what your mind was too preoccupied to notice—there were rapids ahead and you had to be prepared. Open to your heart. Its higher consciousness will whisper to you, warning you of signs of turbulence. It will speak to you through intuition, not reason.

PAULO COELHO

You start by listening, listening to your heart. Then you start to manifest it in the real physical world.

In order to listen to your heart, make time to find peace and quiet. When you're constantly connecting to others by phone, text, or email, you don't give your heart a way to message you. All your circuits are busy and your inner voice can't get through. You're distracted by work or worries and your thoughts get divided into many little bits.

 ISABEL ALLENDE

We can connect to the heart when we are in silence. We live in the noise, and we are so busy all the time, there is no time, no space, no silence for the heart. That is why people meditate or pray, because they need that space, that moment, when you listen to the heart.

We tend to hurry through our days, sometimes feeling trapped and overwhelmed, other times feeling as if we're sleepwalking through our routines. There are plenty of things that we cannot change or even influence: incurable disease, natural disasters, death. But many other things can slip out of our control or escape us because we can't hear the whisperings of our heart above the noise of our mind. When you quiet your mind, you bring it into sync with your heart.

 MICHAEL BECKWITH

If we don't listen to the heart, we'll listen to the chatter of the world, and we will end up walking lockstep in a society of

consumerism, of getting, of fear and of worry, and we will not have lived our life. We have a life to live. The heart has the answers.

Bring your attention to your heart and log on to that all-encompassing, universal server. Its vital information will help you make your life yours to live and allow you to see past your daily responsibilities and short-term goals to your greater purpose.

 JANE GOODALL

If we take the heart out of our consideration, we are making decisions based on "How will this help me now?" and "How will this affect the next shareholders' meeting or the next political campaign?"

Get outside your head in order to hear the voice of your heart. Take time to sit quietly so that you can pull together all these different thoughts and impulses into a single focus. Then you can train your attention on what's important and see yourself and what you're meant to do, where you're meant to go.

 PAULO COELHO

When you listen to your heart, you're able to open the door.

Your mind and attention are like a muscle. Every muscle needs exercise and the kind of exercise your attention needs is quiet focus or mindfulness. This conditions your mind to focus, not fragment. Breathing, walking, or sitting with mindfulness strengthens your awareness so that your mind gets in sync with the beating intelligence of your heart.

> *All who call on God earnestly from the heart will certainly be heard and will receive what they have asked and desired.*
>
> —MARTIN LUTHER

Sometimes what your heart tells you may sound strange or illogical—at first. But don't dismiss these messages out of hand. Sit and listen to them. Try not to analyze them, but judge them by how they feel. The way to the heart is based on feeling. Inspiration from the heart feels organic and natural. Allow the voice to show you what it means. Ask yourself, *How do I feel about this guidance?* You know when a choice is prompted by your heart, because it will feel right to you.

 MAYA ANGELOU

Amazing! I mean you listen to the heart, listen. It may seem frivolous at first, but it needs you. It says, "Come on, I'll show you what you really must do."

If you don't know what to do, do nothing. Don't fill your time with trivia. Simply do nothing. Simply sit. Don't do anything and you may be able to hear your heart.

CONTEMPLATION

Sit and Listen

Sit somewhere quiet to allow your body and mind to get in sync, to be in the same place at the same time. Take three deep, slow breaths in and out to quiet your mind. Bring your attention to your heart so that you can hear your heart, the seat of your soul. As you bring attention to your heart, you gain access to the heart's intelligence. You increase its availability. Your heart becomes adaptable, flexible.

Focus your attention on your breathing as you breathe in and out. If any thoughts and worries come up, allow them to float away as you bring your attention back to your breathing. You are giving your heart space in which to speak to you. Focus only on your in-breath and out-breath . . . Breathe in and out . . .

When you feel quiet, put your attention on your heart. Ask yourself these questions to connect to your heart's energy: *What makes me happy? What do I love to do? What brings me joy? What are my passions? What inspires me and makes me feel fulfilled?*

Now ask yourself what keeps you from connecting with your heart: *What am I spending my time doing that does not make me happy, that keeps me from joy?*

Now ask your heart, *What can I do to get beyond whatever keeps me from connecting with you? What small or big steps can I take? How can I feel inspired and fulfilled?* Open yourself to receiving your heart's answer even if you are afraid of hearing it. Your heart will let you see the truth and help you find your way. Your heart has all the answers.

5. Coherence: Living in the Now

The present moment dies every moment to become the past, is reborn every moment into the future. All experience is now. Now never ends.

—DEEPAK CHOPRA

It's really important *that* your heart beats, but it's also important *how* your heart beats.

The Institute of HeartMath, a leading research institution on the heart and the effects that our hearts have on our lives, has demonstrated a link between your heartbeat and your emotional state. Your heart is much quicker to respond to events around you than your brain is because emotions are faster and more powerful than thoughts. Your heart also reflects your emotional state more than your brain. In other words, when you are scared, nervous, or frustrated, your cardiac rhythm is unstable and irregular. But when you experience love, feel appreciated, or are absorbed in creating something, your cardiac rhythm shows an entirely different pattern. It is calmer and gentler. Scientists refer to this pattern as "heart coherence," and when your heart rhythm is coherent, your body and mind are balanced and in the present. You are physically and mentally at your best, in the now.

Every moment is unique, unknown, completely fresh.

—PEMA CHÖDRÖN

In order to experience heart coherence, you can connect with your heart by doing the simple Inner-ease Exercise on page 47, which the Institute of HeartMath developed.

A coherent rhythm causes all the other systems in our body—the brain and nervous system, the immune and endocrine systems, the digestive and circulatory systems—to function better. When we go into heart-rhythm incoherence because of negative emotions like fear or anger, this has bad effects on our immune system.

 MARCI SHIMOFF

Heart-rhythm coherence is actually our heart's optimal state of func-
tioning. But you can't think your way into coherence—you can't just
think about love and have your heart rhythm sync up. You actually
have to feel the love, feel the gratitude, feel the care, feel the compas-
sion. And that will put you into this optimal state of coherence.

When you connect with your heart, you amplify your positive emotions, which are at the core of your Authentic Power.

The Inner-ease Exercise or Love Response

Step 1: Close your eyes. Put your hand on your heart. This simple act causes a chemical called oxytocin (also known as the "love hormone") to start coursing through your body.

Step 2: Imagine you are breathing in and out through your heart. Exhale more deeply than you inhale, as if gravity is pulling your breath down to the ground. Breathe for six counts in and six counts out, exhaling more deeply than inhaling. Keep doing this until your breathing calms and feels natural.

Step 3: Keep breathing through your heart. On each in-breath, imagine that you're breathing in ease, love, and compassion. Exhale normally. On each in-breath, breathe in ease, love, and compassion. And exhale. With your third inhalation, feel yourself drawing in ease, love, and compassion through your heart. On the exhale, you can take your hand down and open up your eyes.

Notice how you feel in your body right now compared with how you felt a minute ago. Maybe you feel lighter, more relaxed, more at ease. Maybe you have a warm sensation in your heart or even throughout your body.

Do this exercise whenever you can. Try it particularly when you are not feeling too stressed (or when you are actually feeling good). That way, you will become better at using it whenever you are under stress and need to calm down. You can do this with your eyes open after the first time.

If you do this exercise three to five times a day over the next few weeks, you will start to habituate this inner-ease or love response. It will become more and more a habit, so it becomes your default state. Then all you need to do is put your hand up to your heart and the whole process starts automatically.

GARY ZUKAV

How do you connect with your heart? This is the very core of creating Authentic Power. Creating Authentic Power is learning to distinguish love from fear within yourself and choosing love no matter what's happening inside of you or what's going on outside of you.

There are plenty of ways of connecting with your heart and living in the moment. There are as many ways of connecting with the heart as there are people.

 ## ISABEL ALLENDE

My connection is through nature, through my dog. I love to play with a dog. Then I feel my heart exploding and I feel the heat of my heart.

Animals and nature are known to open our hearts, calm us, and reduce blood pressure and stress.

 ## JANE GOODALL

Unless you actually can be out in nature and experience the birds singing in the trees and the blue sky, you are divorced from the great spiritual being that I feel is all around us. And it's being out there in nature. Then you can become a whole human being with heart and brain and spirit all connected and whole.

Jane Goodall *(opposite)*

Many roads lead to the heart. Children tend to be good at following their hearts. Their enthusiasm and intuition lead them until they are told to rein in those impulses. To connect with your heart, it may help you to reconnect with your inner child. Think of what animated you and filled you with joy when you were young. Allow yourself to feel that again, no matter how simple it was—a color, a place, a toy, a food, a game, a visit with a friend or relative. In that lies a connection to your heart.

 PAULO COELHO

To connect to your heart, become a child.

Truly I tell you, unless you change and become like little children, you will never enter the kingdom of heaven.

—JESUS

Reconnecting with your inner child is not the same as behaving in a childish way. It is about allowing your adult self to be guided by your inner child, by that inner voice that, with a gentle whisper, points you in the right direction. The heart reveals the coordinates of your true path. You won't lose your way, even when you seem to be off the beaten track.

 ISABEL ALLENDE

When I'm playing with the kids, when I make love to my husband, when I read a good book, when I'm writing and I feel that

the character becomes a person and talks to me, then my heart also feels "fluttering." I think those are the connections with the heart: creativity, nature, love, prayer, and silence.

Even though people have many different ways of connecting with the heart, the feeling of connectedness is a universal experience. It transcends national borders and links souls around the world. Love connects you with other people. Wherever you are, you will instantly recognize a mother's love for her child—their heart connection is palpable.

 ## MARIANNE WILLIAMSON

On any of the continents anywhere on this planet you see a mother holds her child and takes care of her baby and obviously loves her children. When you're walking anywhere in the world and you see lovers who clearly feel like they have found something special, and you relate to that and you see it, this is the life of the heart.

We can also connect with our hearts by facing difficulties. Our own mortality, the prospect of death, encourages us to listen to our heart and allow its inner voice to speak through any worries or fears. Steve Jobs connected with his heart through awareness of his mortality, which helped him make important decisions. "Because," he reasoned, "almost everything, all external expectations, all pride, all fear of embarrassment or failure, these things just fall away in the face of death, leaving only what is truly important."

There is no reason not to follow your heart.

—STEVE JOBS

 ECKHART TOLLE

How can we connect with the heart? The starting point is: all you ever have is this moment. So you look more deeply into this moment.

The power of the heart is the power of now, of being aware of the moment. Be aware of the abundance of life right now. If you remain stuck in the past, clinging to the baggage of old disappointments or relationships, you block yourself off from the riches of the present. If you worry too much about tomorrow, you can't hear your heart today.

 MICHAEL BECKWITH

In order to tap into the wisdom of the heart, we have to listen. Lowly listening. Ralph Waldo Emerson said, "Be still, turn within and be aware that the answers are not out there somewhere in the world." The answers, the intuitive guidance, the wisdom, it's here.

The answers are in your heart. View your life as a series of present moments. The more you manage to inhale and fully absorb this moment, the better you can hear the voice of your heart.

Michael Beckwith *(opposite)*

 MAYA ANGELOU

I think that it's all you can listen to. I know that with the otic ear, one can listen to the birds, and one can hear the rustle of the leaves of the trees, and the river as it flows, and the ocean as it ebbs and flows. However, to really hear is only with the heart. To hear more than information, it's really wisdom. So that is who you really listen to. And so you become calm, you must become calm.

Reflect on a beautiful moment while you experience it. Allow yourself to appreciate even trivial and ordinary things. See how significant they actually are: a good conversation, a favorite song, a comfortable chair, a ray of sunshine peeking through a blanket of clouds.

As you embrace the present and become one with it, and merge with it, you will experience a fire, a glow, a sparkle of ecstasy. You will become lighthearted, joyous, and free.

—DEEPAK CHOPRA

Seize the day! Play with your child, listen to music, walk in the park, make love, read poetry. Focus on what is good. This keeps you connected to your heart.

 ECKHART TOLLE

To listen to the heart means to be connected with that deepest level within yourself.

The heart is naturally calm and peaceful, clear and strong, the qualities of the deepest level of your consciousness. The closer your connection with your essence, the more loving you will become and the more enjoyment you will derive from everything you encounter on your path.

 GARY ZUKAV

The more you do this, the more the loving parts of your personality and their experiences begin to fill your field of awareness, which means the more loving you become. So that's the way you begin to express your heart.

As Father Matthew Fox says, "If you get cut off from your passion, then where's your compassion going to come from?" Even when you find yourself in difficult or sad circumstances, you can rely on your heart for guidance. As you become better at listening to your heart, it will connect you with other people and communicate options and solutions to you. Allow your heart to open your eyes to something your mind may not have considered. The decision that comes from your heart will always be the right one for you.

Now is all there ever is.

—ECKHART TOLLE

CONTEMPLATION

Present Awareness

Your appointment in life is now, in the present moment. Take a minute to breathe in and out. You can breathe mindfully anywhere—sitting in your car, on the subway or bus, while waiting in a line or walking around the block. Practice the Inner-ease Exercise, or Love Response: Close your eyes. Put your hand on your heart. Imagine you are breathing in and out through your heart. Exhale more deeply than you inhale and breathe in and out six times or until your breathing feels calm and natural. Now, on each in-breath, feel yourself breathing in ease, love, and compassion through your heart. Exhale normally.

Continue to breathe mindfully. Your breathing makes you aware of yourself in the now, wherever you are. With your mind calm from breathing in and out, you can encounter the beautiful things around you right now. View your life as a series of present moments. The past is gone, the future is not here yet. By being in the present, you are in touch with your heart. Listen to what it wants you to hear.

PART 2
The Inner Powers

The power for creating a better future is contained in the present moment: You create a good future by creating a good present.

—ECKHART TOLLE

6. The Power of Gratitude

It is through gratitude for the present moment that
the spiritual dimension of life opens up.

—ECKHART TOLLE

Gratitude, the ability to count your blessings, is the ultimate way to connect with the heart.

 NEALE DONALD WALSCH

I think the heart is gratitude. I think the heart is a feeling. It is the sanctuary for the deepest feelings that can be found within the human experience. And I think among those feelings is the feeling of gratitude. The feeling of being thankful, of being grateful, and of being so in love with life and with everything in life and even, dare I say it, in love with ourselves.

When you are grateful for everything you have, your heart is open. You appreciate the people in your life and they reciprocate. And gratitude creates even more abundance.

 ## MARCI SHIMOFF

People often ask me, "What's the fast track to love?" And there is one answer, I think: "Gratitude." When we're grateful for what's going on in our lives, that is when our heart's open. It's a way that we actually register and savor the good that's going on in our lives.

There is an old saying: "What you appreciate, appreciates." When you appreciate something, then more of that flows into your life.

You can experience gratitude on two different levels: The *first level* of gratitude covers everyday things or interactions. These may range from gratitude for the roof over your head and food for your children to a smile you got from a random passerby on the street. The *second level* of gratitude is to be able to appreciate what you have even after a great loss.

 ## ECKHART TOLLE

Being grateful is another essential part of living in connected-ness with the heart; it comes naturally.

 ## NEALE DONALD WALSCH

Gratitude is an attitude that changes everything. So I tell people that if you really want to use gratitude powerfully, use it even before, not just after, any particular event.

JOE DISPENZA

We usually give thanks for things when they've already happened. So in a sense, we've been hypnotized and conditioned into believing that we need a reason for joy, that we need a reason for gratitude.

Allow yourself to be grateful. Your life will shift into a larger, more positive dimension.

MARCI SHIMOFF

The brain scans of people who are experiencing a state of un-conditional love show that there's actually greater brain activity, that they're more intelligent, that you become more creative. When you're feeling more gratitude or you're forgiving people, that's increasing your intelligence.

To increase your awareness of everything that merits gratitude and to make yourself more receptive to the beautiful and loving things in life, keep a gratitude diary. Start each day by writing down a minimum of five things you are grateful for. People who regularly record what they are grateful for are happier than others—and their happiness lasts. Keeping a gratitude diary works even better than therapy or antidepressant drugs.

HOWARD MARTIN

It's very, very simple: the more we appreciate, the more we gain. Appreciation is a heart-related feeling. It requires access to the

*intelligence of the heart to appreciate or to have gratitude, espe-
cially when things don't go your way. To find something in those
times when life is tough, to appreciate something about them or
appreciate something about something else, it begins to shift the
energies very, very quickly so that you come into another level of
buoyancy that rises above the problem. And in doing so, you can
then see into it. You can then find ways to deal with it.*

With the *second level* of gratitude, you give thanks even in the face of
major disappointments, like the breakdown of a love affair, the loss of
a job, and even in the face of great sadness or tragedy, like the death
of a loved one. This gratitude helps you pave the way for a new life.
Even out of the worst thing that ever happened to you—an illness or
disability or terrible loss—eventually can come new understanding,
new connections, and relationships.

 ## RUEDIGER SCHACHE

*If you express yourself in appreciation or in gratitude, it's like
sending love to God, sending love out in the universe. Gratitude
is opening the heart.*

 ## PAULO COELHO

*At the end of the day, when your heart is open, there is this
energy of love that fulfills everything.*

MICHAEL BECKWITH

When you begin to live at that level, the universe responds to that field, and then more and more and more things to be grateful for show up out of nothing.

There is love in everyone, always waiting for the moment it can free itself, like a butterfly from its cocoon. You release love within yourself by appreciating life and the people around you. That love you send out will come back to you many times over, attracting people, ideas, and events that enrich your life.

Deep listening requires letting go of our internal argument with the world. We must exhaust ourselves of our assumptions.

—MARK NEPO

 MARCI SHIMOFF

That perspective helps us keep our hearts open in a state of love. And living in a state of gratitude, living in the belief that this is a friendly universe changes everything. We move from feeling afraid and challenged to feeling open and looking at life through the eyes of love, through the eyes of the heart.

CONTEMPLATION

Three Blessings

In general, we think too much about what goes wrong and not enough about what goes right. To be healthier and happier, we can think more about what has gone well and exercise gratitude. Positive psychologist Martin Seligman created this exercise, which increases happiness and well-being in everyone who tries it.

WHAT WENT WELL, OR THREE BLESSINGS

Every night for a week, take ten minutes before you go to sleep to write down three things that went well for you today. Keep a physical record in a journal or on your computer or your phone's notes app. The three things that went well can be small or large, unimportant or important. ("The train came on time." "My husband cleared the snow from the driveway." "My niece's surgery was successful." "My boss gave our department a bonus.")

Next to each item that went well, answer the question "Why did this go well?" ("The train crews anticipated bad weather." "My husband can be thoughtful." "My niece found the right doctor and prepared for her surgery." "Our department works hard and well together.")

Keep this list for at least one week and you will feel better, happier, and more grateful for all the blessings in your life. You will feel more connected to your heart and your life in the present. The longer you practice gratitude and counting your blessings, the longer your happiness will last and the more blessings you will have.

7. Becoming a Person of the Heart

When you begin to touch your heart or let your heart be touched, you begin to discover that it's bottomless . . . huge, vast, and limitless.

—PEMA CHÖDRÖN

Because Eckhart Tolle's words had set me on my path to exploring the powers of the heart, I was particularly eager to meet and interview him. I also wanted to hear about Tolle's own awakening experience as a young research assistant at the University of Cambridge. At his home near Vancouver, Canada, Tolle told me that in his twenties, he wrestled for years with unbearable anxiety and thoughts of suicide. The world felt cold and hostile to him and he reached the point where he felt he wanted to leave it sooner rather than later. One night, the pain, anxiety, and dread were worse than ever before, and Tolle kept thinking that he just could not live with himself anymore.

Suddenly, he had a different thought: "If I cannot live with myself, then there must be two selves: the 'I' and the 'self' that 'I' cannot live with." And, he realized, perhaps only one of those selves was real.

This realization so overwhelmed Tolle that in that moment, he was unable to think anymore. Even though he was conscious, his mind could not form a single thought; for the first time in his life, his mind was put completely on standby. He wanted to breathe a sigh of relief, but before he could, he suddenly felt drawn into a vortex of energy and his body began to tremble uncontrollably. Scared that he might lose himself, Tolle clung desperately to who he thought himself to be: Ulrich Leonard Tolle, a research assistant, a German, a man, a person, a . . . But all he could do was to give in to that whirl of energy. When he did, he heard a voice within his chest tell him not to resist—and suddenly he wasn't afraid.

Tolle could not remember what happened next, but when he came to the next morning, he felt different. At peace. And the world around him seemed to have changed. It no longer seemed hostile, but beautiful. Tolle strolled through the city in utter amazement at the beauty all around him. He felt as if he had been born again in some essential way.

Only later would he understand what had happened to him. The intense pressure of his suffering that night had become so bad that his consciousness had been forced to liberate itself from his unhappy and fearful "self." Tolle said it was as if his past had been suddenly erased and his future had become unimportant. The only thing that mattered was the present, the now. And in that powerful here and now, everything was good.

Eckhart Tolle *(opposite)*

Wherever you are, be there totally. If you find your here and now intolerable and it makes you unhappy, you have three options: remove yourself from the situation, change it, or accept it totally. If you want to take responsibility for your life, you must choose one of those three options, and you must choose now. Then you must accept the consequences.

—ECKHART TOLLE, *THE POWER OF NOW*

In his new state of consciousness, Tolle realized he only needed to be himself. His true purpose was to be in the present. According to Tolle, we all can reach this state of consciousness, of being in the now, of pulling body and soul together into one consciousness when we shut down the noise of our thoughts. Then we are able to connect with our heart, the conduit to our true, essential selves. By focusing your awareness on your heart, by listening to the voice of your heart, you get an understanding of who you really are.

You are more than your name, nationality, profession, or any other label. Even if you were to adopt a different name or change your nationality or profession, you would remain yourself. You're also more than your personality, whether you're kind or competitive, optimistic or fatalistic. You're also more than your physical body. If you are seriously injured, you may change in some ways, but you are essentially the same individual.

DEAN SHROCK

If I could create a new diagnostic code, I would actually call it Forgotten Identity. I think we've genuinely forgotten who we really are and the power we have and our real essence.

Your true identity is your heart, the seat of your soul, the most authentic, most genuine, and most profound core of yourself. Your heart and soul are your essence. Your personality operates in the world of your five senses, but you don't perceive your soul with those senses. Your soul is beyond the world of labels.

> *Living up to an image that you have of yourself or that other people have of you is inauthentic living.*
>
> —ECKHART TOLLE, *A NEW EARTH*

Yet, to live in the world, we modify our behavior to fit all kinds of situations: at home, at work, at school, at the gym. As we do, we may project an image of ourselves, a persona that is at odds with our true selves. This personality can make us afraid to be as we really are, so sometimes we deny our true selves and hide behind a mask.

 ## DEEPAK CHOPRA

Every child has played hide-and-seek. And you know when you play hide-and-seek, there is a part of you that doesn't want to be found out and there is another part of you that wants to be found out. So we lose ourselves and ultimately we find ourselves. That's the play of life.

In a way you spend your whole life playing hide-and-seek. On the one hand, you hope not to be found, because you are comfortable with the personality you've assumed. On the other hand, you want to be found, because, deep down, your personality chafes against your true self. To resolve this discrepancy, align your personality with your soul.

MARIANNE WILLIAMSON

That shift from body identification to spirit identification, that is the meaning of enlightenment. And that is the same thing as saying "going from the perceptions of the mind to the knowledge of the heart."

By shifting your attention from your head to your heart, you connect with your true self and develop the courage to be who you really are.

 MARCI SHIMOFF

When we look at life through the eyes of love and through the eyes of the heart, everything changes. The world outside may or may not change, or may not appear to our liking, but when we change how we're perceiving it, when we move from our thoughts to the feelings of love, everything in the world around us appears different.

When we look at the world only through our thoughts, through our minds, it can seem difficult or hostile. We have 60,000 thoughts a day and 80 percent are negative, but when we drop our attention into the heart and we start living more from the heart, life appears different. The world looks different.

 MARCI SHIMOFF

Instead of a negative place, it becomes a friendly universe. Einstein said that the most important question a person can ask

himself is "Is this a friendly universe?" and the people who are
happiest answer, "Yes, this is a friendly universe." That doesn't
mean that everything is always going your way. What it means
is you believe that this is a universe that is on your side.

There is nothing either good or bad but thinking makes it so.

—WILLIAM SHAKESPEARE, *HAMLET*

Keeping your heart open keeps you connected to your essence. Your true self is effectively a universal self, your true identity, part of something much bigger that we might call the "soul of the world." You are your soul first and your body second. Your body is merely an envelope that enables you to function in the physical world, whereas your soul transcends all the sensory perceptions, dimensions, and other elements of that physical world.

Just by being ourselves, we are borne toward a destiny far beyond
anything we could imagine. The Being I nourish inside me is the same as
the Being that suffuses every atom of the cosmos.

—DEEPAK CHOPRA, *UNCONDITIONAL LIFE*

Staying aligned with your heart and soul connects you to the universe.

Human beings are made of body, mind, and spirit. Of these,
spirit is primary, for it connects us to the source of everything,
the eternal field of Consciousness.

—DEEPAK CHOPRA, *THE SEVEN SPIRITUAL LAWS FOR PARENTS*

ECKHART TOLLE

You reach God not by reaching out, which for thousands of years most humans have done when they talked about God. Their eyes would go upward and you would look for God up there somewhere, but nobody ever found God up there. There was even a Russian astronaut who came back from space and said, "I didn't see any God up there." And of course he didn't, because God is the divine dimension that is the essence of who you are, and that is heart. The heart of the universe, the heart of who you are.

There is no difference between your true self and somebody else's. We are all connected. As Tolle writes in *The Power of Now*, "You just can't feel it because your mind is making too much noise."

 # NEALE DONALD WALSCH

In my awareness, in my deep understanding, all of us are man-ifestations of the divine. That is, each of us is a singularization of God itself. And I think the experience of that occurs when our hearts crack wide open. And we see our true identity, we see to the deepest part of who we are.

From the moment you come into being, you are your soul. Your soul gets all the vital functions going. And because your soul is immaterial, it cannot die. Your personality will die, but your soul will live on.

Dr. Kathy Magliato, a cardiothoracic surgeon who writes about the heart's many meanings, frequently witnesses patients' final heartbeats as they move between life and death. "Something very definite, very distinct leaves their body when their heart stops," she says, and she believes this is their soul. She also believes "that the soul resides in the heart," because once the heart stops, the soul departs.

> *It is only to the individual that a soul is given.*
>
> —ALBERT EINSTEIN, "SCIENCE AND RELIGION"

Your soul, your universal self, adopts an earthly personality. Your personality tends to emphasize the differences between you and others, but when you recognize that you are a spiritual being having a human experience, that we are all spiritual beings, you see the connectedness and realize that you are first and foremost a soul.

 GARY ZUKAV

Instead of being insignificant and powerless, you begin to glimpse something, something that can be terrifying at first—that you are a compassionate, loving, powerful, and creative spirit.

You are here to live from the heart.

CONTEMPLATION

A Sense of Soul on Earth

With an open heart, you see the world in beautiful detail—friendly, spacious, alive. Every detail has its own place and meaning, writes physicist and mindfulness teacher Jeremy Hayward, in *Sacred World: The Shambhala Way to Gentleness, Bravery, and Power,* in which he also offers this contemplation.

To heighten your heart's perceptions, think of or look at something beautiful, say, a flower. Notice the whole flower, its color and shape. Look closer and see smaller details: veins in the petals and leaves, the center's delicate texture. Enter into the space of those details, feel the vastness inside and around each. Connect to the space inside and around the flower.

Now connect to the space around you. Lie down on the floor or bed and pull your body into a tight ball in the classic fetal position. Pull your knees up to your chest, put your arms around them, head over your knees. Close your eyes tight and feel black space all around you. Tense all the muscles in your body from your feet, through your legs and back, up through your head. Hold that tension a little while. Keeping your eyes closed, gradually relax each muscle, toe to head. Trust that the world is good. Keep your eyes closed and let yourself come out of this ball and slowly unfold until you are sitting on the floor.

Now open your eyes. Breathe out. Feel the air on your skin and the space around you. Look around you at one thing at a time. Look closely and notice not just each object but the space and light around it. Take your time with each object around you and feel the goodness of what you see.

8. Creating Authentic Power

Be kind, for everyone you meet is fighting a great battle.

—PHILO OF ALEXANDRIA

Mindfulness teacher Thich Nhat Hanh tells a story about the Buddha. The night before his awakening, he was attacked by an army that shot thousands of arrows at him. But as the arrows arched toward the Buddha, they turned into flowers and fell harmlessly at his feet. Understanding and compassion help us transform negative emotions into harmless ones, into awareness. This is Authentic Power.

You must find the place inside yourself where nothing is impossible.

—DEEPAK CHOPRA, *THE THIRD JESUS*

Picture your heart and soul as the mother ship of a large fleet. Your personality is one of the many ships accompanying it, but, ultimately, only one ship, the mother ship, knows where the entire fleet is headed and can stay the course. When you follow your heart, aligning your personality with your soul, you exercise Authentic Power. You feel on course. You feel joy, meaning, and purpose. You are aware of your energy, thoughts, and inner guidance. Whenever you are off course, you feel unhappy.

 GARY ZUKAV

The pain in your life is a measure of the distance between your current self-perception and the reality of yourself as a powerful and compassionate, creative and loving spirit. Closing that distance to zero is the spiritual path. It is now the evolutionary requirement for each of us to create Authentic Power.

Where love rules, there is no will to power; and where power predominates, there love is lacking. The one is the shadow of the other.

—CARL JUNG

The four fundamental properties of Authentic Power are

- *Love:* This kind of love includes compassion, caring about others. This kind of love makes you view every hungry mother and every hungry child as your own mother and your own child.
- *Humility:* This kind of humility recognizes that the lives of others can be just as difficult as your own, that everyone goes through life with some pain, loss, and difficulty. Humility allows you to bear in mind that everybody is a beautiful soul and that everybody struggles.

- *Forgiveness:* Forgiving someone for hurting or wronging you is like laying down a heavy burden. The person you forgive may not even be aware of your action, because you do it first and foremost for yourself. Unless you forgive, you will find yourself looking at the world as if through a pair of dark glasses that makes everything look dreary and adversarial. Forgiving is like taking off those glasses and seeing that the world is full of love and light.
- *Clarity:* Clarity is seeing your life as part of a greater whole. You realize that you are not a victim, but that you are here on earth to learn from all of your experiences, both positive and negative. You realize that you are an immortal soul and thus infinitely more than just the body and personality you possess at present.

Day-to-day life often unfolds in a kind of competition between personalities—lovers, spouses, parents, siblings, businesses, social classes, and nations. All try to exert control over one another. Called external power, this control is based on our senses—what we can see, hear, smell, taste, or touch in the external world. Unlike Authentic Power, it is competitive and seeks to have the upper hand.

Power over others is weakness disguised as strength.

—ECKHART TOLLE, *THE POWER OF NOW*

GARY ZUKAV

External power is the old way of understanding power. It's what enabled us to survive, yes. And to evolve since our origin as a species, yes. But it doesn't work any longer. It's counterproductive

81

to our evolution. It's toxic and it is being replaced. Correction: it has been replaced with another understanding of power.

Everything you obtain at the expense of someone else is a manifestation of external power, which operates on the principle that "one man's breath is another man's death." Things you are scared of losing, like your house, car, looks, and sharp mind are all examples of external power. Relying on these impermanent things makes you vulnerable.

 LINDA FRANCIS

External power comes and goes. You can earn it; you can lose it. You can inherit it; it can get stolen.

To move from external power to Authentic Power, listen to the voice of your heart, the seat of your soul. Align your personality with your essential loving qualities.

 GARY ZUKAV

Authentic Power is the experience of joy, of meaning, of purpose, of fulfillment, of being in the right place at the right time. Of knowing that your life has a purpose and what you are doing is contributing to that purpose. It is the alignment of your personality with your soul, with harmony and cooperation and sharing and reverence for life.

Authentic Power recognizes meaning and purpose in the smallest things.

Linda Francis (opposite)

ECKHART TOLLE

Authentic Power is not personal power. It is a power that far transcends who you think yourself to be as a person. It is a power that lies at the very heart—not just of yourself—but of the very heart of the universe. So if you are connected with that level within yourself, you're not just connected with the essence of who you are, but you're also connected with the very essence of the universe. And that is pointed to in the ancient dictum, "As above, so below."

To create Authentic Power, it helps to become aware of any emotions that keep you invested in external power. Because your feelings and emotions are the force field in which your soul operates, you have to become aware of your emotions in order to align your personality with your soul.

 GARY ZUKAV

Instead of looking outward to create external power, to manipulate or to control others, you look inward to see the internal origins of your experiences.

You can do this by focusing on what happens in your body when a negative emotion crops up, with a technique called Emotional Awareness.

 LINDA FRANCIS

I've got great news for you. Every emotion that you have, every single emotion that you have, is a message from your soul. That is exciting.

It's powerful to know that because if you know that, then you'll pay attention. You would want to pay attention to a message from your soul. I know you would.

Each and every emotion is like a spontaneous text message from your inner source. It is important not to delete these texts from the soul, but to notice, register, and absorb them. Your heart is the cell phone that receives your soul's text messages. With an open heart, you can face up to fears and nourish loving emotions.

DEAN SHROCK

Our emotions actually function like a guidance system to let us know when we are resonating with our core essence and love. And so, honestly, by simply paying attention to how you feel, you can know whether or not you're doing what is honestly right for you, what works for you.

Your emotions will let you know right away whether you are on the right track in aligning your personality and life with your soul.

ISABEL ALLENDE

How do I know if something is good for me or good for the world? It's my body that tells me how I feel it, and I think that the heart is the center of that.

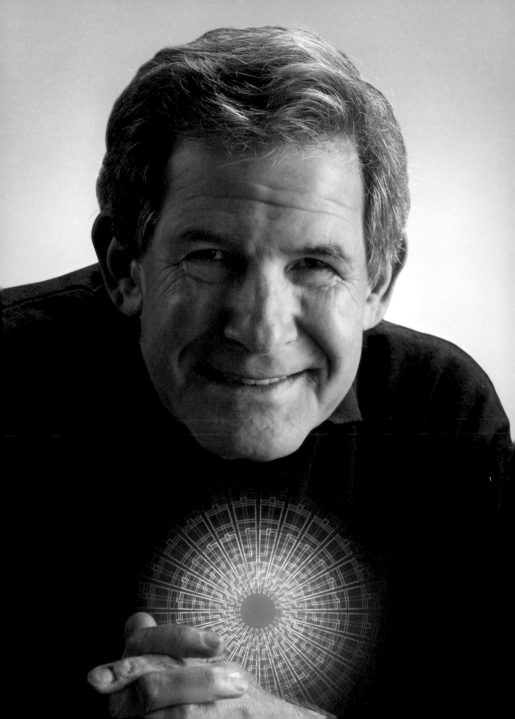

LINDA FRANCIS

Emotional awareness is a tool that I use to create Authentic Power, to grow spiritually. And it is a way that I am able to detect in myself, physically, energy centers in my body. I check inside all the time. I notice what's happening physically, the sensations that are going on in my throat area or my heart or my solar plexus and in other energy centers. So I can tell whether I have fear-based parts of my personality or love-based parts of my personality active.

Your body constantly reflects your emotional state. Notice the ways that your emotions reveal themselves physically. Make a habit of asking yourself why, in a certain state of mind, you feel something in your body. Consider whether it feels good to you, or not. There is a reason stress makes you uncomfortable and positive emotions produce happiness.

 GARY ZUKAV

Emotional awareness doesn't just mean the ability to say, "I'm angry or I'm sad, or I'm happy." No, it's more precise and grounded and much more accurate than that. It means being able to look inside your body at specific areas, for example your throat area, your chest area, and your solar plexus area, and others as well, and see what physical sensations you can detect there.

If there are uncomfortable sensations or painful sensations, then you know that a frightened part of your personality is active. That means a part of your personality that comes from fear

Gary Zukav *(opposite)*

and the behaviors of that part of your personality will be things like anger, jealousy, resentment, feeling superior and entitled, feeling inferior and needing to please.

And once you know that, you know that acting in love will create constructive and beneficial experiences for you, and good-feeling experiences for you. And acting in fear will create painful and destructive experiences for you. It's a matter of emotional awareness and responsible choice.

With love, clarity, wisdom, you create Authentic Power. With Authentic Power, you can see past an emotion and into another person's soul. You do not judge or condemn. You align your personality with your soul and use the power of your heart.

 ## LINDA FRANCIS

Creating Authentic Power actually means I'm cultivating loving parts of my personality, the parts that appreciate life, the parts that experience joy, the parts that experience compassion.

 ## GARY ZUKAV

The heart of it all is love. Love. Living your life with an empowered heart without attachment to the outcome. The intention is the quality of consciousness that infuses your actions. If it is an energy of fear, it will be an energy of needing to dominate, needing to control, needing to manipulate. That is attachment

to the outcome. If it is an energy of love, it will be the energy
of care, of patience, of kindness, of consideration, of gratitude.

With Authentic Power, you can see everything that comes your way as a gift of sorts or a necessary lesson. You can accept that not every gift looks positive when you first receive it.

> *Be grateful for whoever comes, because each has*
> *been sent as a guide from beyond.*
>
> —RUMI

Many difficulties or challenges—even illnesses and tragedies—have no apparent silver lining when they occur. But you can be grateful to be alive even in the face of a terrible loss and eventually come to terms with it. What do you still have in your life, in spite of your loss? Are you able to do good for others as a result of coming through a crisis?

 ECKHART TOLLE

No matter what you achieve outwardly in this world, you will always
very quickly encounter frustration, disappointment, and some form
of unhappiness or suffering, despite all your achievements, if you are
not living in connectedness with that deepest level within yourself.

However successful your personality is in everyday life—with an impressive career, luxury goods, prestigious address—as long as you are not exercising Authentic Power, your success will not bring you satisfaction.

NEALE DONALD WALSCH

If we ignore matters of the heart or if we do not consult the heart, as we move through the experiences of life, then we wind up with a series of events leading us nowhere. But if we follow the advice of the heart, if we seek the counsel of the heart, then we wind up with a series of experiences that take us back home.

 ## GARY ZUKAV

As you create Authentic Power, your life begins to fill with meaning, and purpose, and vitality, and creativity, because you are moving in the direction that your soul wants you to go.

You can use every new experience to align your personality with your soul. Every situation gives you the opportunity to approach life with an open heart, conveying love to the world. That is the purpose of the human experience you have as a spiritual being. That is the reason for your existence. That is Authentic Power.

> *What lies behind us and what lies before us are tiny matters compared to what lies within us.*
>
> —OLIVER WENDELL HOLMES

CONTEMPLATION

Calm by Looking Deeply

Zen master Thich Nhat Hanh teaches us that, whenever you become aware of a strong, troubling, or negative emotion, you can calm yourself by focusing your mind on your breathing. Putting attention on your breathing, in and out, you calm down. Just concentrate on breathing from the abdomen. Breathing in, feel your belly rise. Breathing out, feel your belly fall. Breathe in with your mind on your breathing—is it fast and short or deep and slow? Breathe in and out mindfully to calm your breathing.

When your breathing is deep and slow, breathe in and be aware that your strong emotion is subsiding. Breathing out you feel that any anger or fear is ebbing. Breathing in, you feel that your emotion has passed. Breathing out, you feel that your emotion has passed. Stay in the long moment of peace. Now you can see beyond the emotion. You are aware of your deep connection to the person or situation that gave rise to the emotion and now you can act with Authentic Power, with awareness of your soul connection.

9. The Powers of Intention and Intuition

It is more important to be of pure intention than of perfect action.

—ILYAS KASSAM

Everything you do, as well as everything you think, originates in a certain intention. Your intention not only rules your life but it also determines the outcome of all your actions.

ECKHART TOLLE

Whatever situation you find yourself in, a very important question to ask yourself is "What is my intention here? What is my primary intention?" In other words, what really matters first of

all at any given moment, and no matter what you are doing, is,
What is your state of consciousness out of which you act?

Deep in your heart you know what the intention is that feeds your actions or thoughts. Only you can know. And you know whether what you are doing is aimed at harmony and cooperation or at personal gain only.

 ## MAYA ANGELOU

You may intend to have a million dollars, and that intention will need you to rob a bank or to mug somebody in the street. Your intention might be to have this woman: "I want this woman, I want this man for my man." However, if we really want the thing, go to the heart and say, "This is what I want." And the heart can say, "Well, I'll help you to get it. I'll show you how to get it. You must be willing to work now. Trust me now and then you can have it. Yes, if it is not going to hurt anyone else. Yes."

The intention underlying your actions and thoughts is energy. Any energy you expend always comes back to you, either directly or indirectly. So you want to act with that in mind. You want to act mindfully, from the heart, with love, and Right Intention.

 ## ISABEL ALLENDE

I have to act from a place of good intention, a place of love and kindness. It's a place of good intention that will allow me to walk in this world, without creating any damage.

Maya Angelou *(opposite)*

If you radiate genuine love and compassion, you will ultimately receive love and compassion back. If, on the other hand, you radiate fear and suspicion, you will encounter situations full of fear and suspicion. It is simplistic to say that, if you are angry today, you will attract angry people tomorrow, but, if you are generally rather tough and distrustful, you will in the long term attract people who have those personalities and attitudes. You are attracted to people with the same energy, and you attract people who experience the world as you do. They understand you and you understand them. You could say that you receive from the world what you give to the world. So your intention is a cause that gives rise to the same effects.

 ECKHART TOLLE

Your primary intention needs to be your state of consciousness at this moment. Your intention needs to be connectedness with the heart at this moment.

What you mean is what you get. Once you decide to live in connectedness with your heart, you experience a different, more positive reality. Because your intention originates in your heart, it enables you to attract the energy of harmony and love. Your intention is the quality of consciousness that infuses your actions.

The intention at the root of your actions matters. The energy of your intention influences the consequences of your actions. Every word you speak and everything you do is infused with consciousness. If you think in terms of giving, you will attract like-minded souls with whom you create a reality of generosity, a reality that reflects that intention. This may well be one of the greatest truths of the universe, which is sometimes called karma.

If I create from the heart, nearly everything works;
if from the head, almost nothing.

—MARC CHAGALL

Of course, there will always be unpleasant things in life that you cannot influence, which are out of your control. However, there are also plenty of things that slip out of your control because you are not fully aware of the intention underlying your actions. That is why it is important to be mindful of the energy you create.

Every significant vital sign—body temperature, heart rate, oxygen consumption, hormone level, brain activity, and so on—alters the moment you decide to do anything . . . Decisions are signals telling your body, mind, and environment to move in a certain direction.

—DEEPAK CHOPRA, *THE BOOK OF SECRETS*

Whenever you feel that your life is slipping out of control, that you are being manipulated by those around you, that things are not going your way, choose to think and act with a positive intention and positive mind-set. Think of good ways in which to look at your situation. You're more likely to find opportunities that you would otherwise have missed.

The time is always right to do what is right.

—MARTIN LUTHER KING JR.

Choosing to create an intention that has loving consequences calls for more than just saying that you are choosing that intention. You have to feel that energy in your heart. The universe looks straight through a false intention to see what is in your heart. Listen to your heart to discover what you really intend to achieve with your actions. Connect with your heart to create the energy of positive, right intention.

 GARY ZUKAV

This is at the heart of creating Authentic Power, learning to distinguish your intentions. The intentions that come from fear are attached to an outcome. In order to be satisfied, they must have that outcome. Those parts of your personality must manipulate and control circumstances and people to their satisfaction. The parts of your personality that originate in love, care about people. They care about others.

Love without action is meaningless and action without love is irrelevant.

—DEEPAK CHOPRA

When you do something for personal gain, your intention is coming from fear, from your personality. When you act to create harmony and cooperation, your intention is from your heart. Your heart and soul have only loving properties. Only the intentions that originate in your heart can lend your life true fulfillment and meaning.

 MAYA ANGELOU

If you speak from the heart, your intention will be heartful, will be wise.

Zen teacher Thich Nhat Hanh suggests that we practice asking several questions to make sure we are creating right or good intentions. You might even want to write these questions on a piece of paper and put it where you will encounter it as you go through your day. Before you pose these questions, take three slow breaths in and out so that you come into the present moment.

The first question to ask yourself before you act is "Am I sure?" or "What am I doing?" This can help you head off wrong perceptions so that you make sure you know what you are doing and where you are going before you act. Then ask, "Is my intention right for now?" Next, ask yourself, "Am I acting automatically or out of habit?" The energy of habit can sometimes be unconscious rather than intentional, so you want to be mindful of both your intention and your action. Finally, ask yourself, "Is my intention based in loving-kindness, in compassion and well-wishes for others?"

These questions can help you become aware of your intentions and actions.

Your Intuition's Language

Intuition is really a sudden immersion of the soul into
the universal current of life.

—PAULO COELHO, *THE ALCHEMIST*

There is no denying intuition. Even extremely rational, commonsensical people can think of moments when they were helped by intuition. In fact, Aristotle defined wisdom as "intuitive reason combined with scientific knowledge."

Our five senses enable us to perceive a part of physical reality—we see, hear, taste, smell, and touch the world around us. But inevitably we come up against the limits of our five senses and rational thought. That is when we must connect with the heart and its intuitive power in order to know what to do.

You cannot hear the voice of your heart with your ears or indeed with any of your other senses. For that you need intuition, a form of perception that transcends sensory perception.

 LINDA FRANCIS

Five-sensory perception is everything you can experience with your five senses. Everything you can see, like the ocean, everything you can hear, everything you can touch, everything you can smell, like a chocolate cake baking in the oven, everything you can taste, like a strawberry or a mango. Now we have access to more than the five senses, to another bigger sensory system that can give us information that our eyes and ears and nose and taste and touch cannot usually give us.

Your heart gives you access to multisensory perceptions—your intuition—just as it connects you with the universe and the higher level of your consciousness. Intuition is intangible but also very personal. No two people on earth have the same fingerprints, and the same holds true for intuition: no two people's intuition works in the same way. Every human being has his or her own distinct intuition, which is fed by the emotions.

Intuition is the heart's language. You can find out how your intuition works by directing your attention inward, just as you look inward to connect with your heart.

 ## GARY ZUKAV

Imagine you have spent the day hiking in a mountainous country. And now you realize you don't know where you are. And it's getting dark, and it's getting cold, and you are shivering. Now it's getting darker, so dark that you can't see anything at all. But you hear strange sounds: "Ooooh. Is that an owl?" You see a dark shape: "Oooh, was that an animal? Was that a bear?" But something inside you says, "It's okay, you are okay. This is a good place to be." But you're hungry, and your stomach is growling. You need to get home. And something inside you says, "That's okay, you're all right." But people are worried about you and you need to find your car immediately. And again something inside you says, "It's all right, you're okay, you're okay." You lie down and you try to sleep. At last, the sun rises and you see almost in front of you a steep cliff and you are at the top of it. If you had gone just a few feet more, you would have fallen over the cliff. The rising dawn shows you what could have taken your life. The voice inside you, the one that said, "It's okay, this is a good place to be," saw everything. It saw the cliff. It knows exactly where you need to go and why. That is multisensory perception.

By opening your heart, you tap into your intuition, which lets you perceive a nonvisible reality that you cannot discern with your five senses. Whereas your senses can be misled, your intuition will never let you down.

 ## LINDA FRANCIS

This is the voice of the soul speaking to you. It tells you many more things than how to stay alive. It tells you where friends and colleagues are waiting, what paths to avoid, and what paths to explore. It always guides you, and supports you, and takes you toward meaning. Multisensory perception is the experience and the knowing that goes beyond the five senses.

 ## PAULO COELHO

It is very important to listen to our heart, not because we have all the answers there—we may have all the answers there—but somehow the heart is provoking in us something that we have lost, and that is our intuition. And based on our intuition, we can move ahead.

Your own intuition or multisensory perception has a unique voice or feeling.

 ## LINDA FRANCIS

There are so many ways to recognize multisensory perception. If you had that thought, that everything is perfect, that's it. If you sense for a moment that a coincidence is more than a coincidence, that there is something powerful and meaningful behind it, that's it.

 GARY ZUKAV

You begin to find that you know things, or you have a sense that you know things about other people. For example, you see someone in the supermarket. And you have a sense that she has just been divorced, and she is in a lot of pain. That's it. Or that someone who appears rough and intimidating has a kind heart. That's it.

Your heart's intuition also allows you to see beneath the surface of other people's behavior, to exercise compassion. For example, when someone seems upset with you, your intuition may allow you to see that this person is under stress that causes him to project his frustration onto you.

 LINDA FRANCIS

There's a big way, if you begin to sense that you are more than you thought you were, that you are more than a mind in a body. That's it. It is beginning to see more. It is beginning to see all that you have seen before, all that your five senses can reveal to you. And at the same time realizing there is intelligence and purpose and power behind it. That's multisensory perception.

This creative force of the imagination is part of the heart's constant generativity, always offering you new opportunities. Your heart offers you these opportunities through your intuition, so you can approach life in a different, fuller way.

ISABEL ALLENDE

My body can only perceive certain things, but there is much more to that reality. When I write, when I've enough time alone and in silence, I can see, I can perceive those connections between the things of the past and the future. I can relate events, cause and effect, in ways that I don't when I am busy, and when I'm in the noise, and when I am with other people.

People say that I write in the style of magic realism, whatever that is, as if it was some kind of literary device, a style. That is the way I conduct my life. The world is a very mysterious place and we know very little. There are dimensions of reality, and maybe everything happens simultaneously and everything from the past or the future is happening in this very moment in this place.

So writing has been my spiritual pathway of finding out where the soul is. And I can perceive things that other people think are sort of crazy. For example, I dream a lot and write down the dreams, because it's my soul telling me something that I need to pay attention to.

Intuition always has your best interests at heart and favors loving impulses and intentions. Whenever you are in doubt, act from the heart.

The intuitive mind is a sacred gift and the rational mind is a faithful servant.

—ALBERT EINSTEIN

Isabel Allende *(opposite)*

 GARY ZUKAV

Intellectual understanding does not disappear with the emergence of multisensory perception. It becomes demoted. It's no longer the chairman of the board, it becomes an employee. It is now at the service of the heart.

JOE DISPENZA

When we begin to open our heart, we're actually functioning from a different level of consciousness. Where we place our attention is where we place our energy. The heart begins to pick up intuitive information. And the heart receives intuitive information before the brain does.

Everything in life is connected. Your intuition allows you to see those connections all around you and act in concert with them.

We always know which is the best road to follow, yet we often follow only the road we have become accustomed to. Once you've connected to your heart, you can act on your intuition, your highest form of intelligence, without needing to question it or know why.

The power of intuitive understanding will protect you from harm until the end of your days.

—LAO TZU

CONTEMPLATION

Following Your Intuition

Your intuition speaks to you in its own way. It may make you feel uncomfortable or irritable in order to get your attention. It might make you anxious or give you a feeling of detachment, as if you've suddenly lost touch with your feelings and need to reconnect. It may communicate to you in a dream or a song that you can't get out of your head—maybe there is a literal or metaphoric message in the dream or lyric. Maybe you hear an inner voice that delivers actual words of warning or direction. Or you get a certain feeling in your body, a sense of knowing—a pit in your stomach or a lightness in your head.

If you think of someone out of the blue, send him an email or give her a call. Pay attention to first impressions you have to situations and first responses to questions that cross your mind. Keep a journal of your intuitions and what happens when you act on them.

However your intuition communicates to you, trust it. Give it your attention. Sit with it; relax into it. Be open to what it tells you. Don't argue with your intuition even if it's telling you some-thing you don't want to hear. Follow its guidance as best you can. It may not be logical and it may not give you the whole picture of what is going to happen all at once. You may have to follow it and allow events to unfold before you see how accurate it is.

10. Synchronicity: The Hidden Order Behind Everything

There are no mistakes, no coincidences. All events are blessings given to us to learn from.

—ELISABETH KÜBLER-ROSS

A few months after I had started working on the film, *The Power of the Heart*, I began to have serious doubts about what I was doing. I wasn't at all sure that I could pull off such an ambitious project. For a while, I even thought about quitting altogether and going back to working as a lawyer—after all, that's what I had been trained to do.

Unable to stand these doubts anymore, one day I said to myself, *If I am really supposed to be doing this, if this is what life wants from me, then I need a signal, a confirmation—and I need it* today. I even found myself saying this out loud to the universe: "If I am supposed to do this, give me a sign!"

Moments later, the doorbell rang. The mailman greeted me and handed me a pile of magazines. The headline on the magazine on top read, in big letters, *Follow Your Heart.* (*Volg je Hart* in Dutch).

At that point I knew that this was the sign I needed. I was flooded by a deep sense of gratitude—and I had no more doubts!

There is a greater power behind absolutely everything you do. Things happen for a reason, and when it seems as if the world is working with you, not against you, that is synchronicity. Haven't you had the feeling that something was not "just" a coincidence? Maybe you heard song lyrics on the radio that resonated throughout your day. Or you thought of a friend you hadn't seen in a long time and at that very moment she called you with great news.

 GARY ZUKAV

Synchronicity is this interesting, funny-sounding word that was created by Carl Jung. And what he meant by it was those times in your life when something appears to be a coincidence but you know that there is more to it than that. There is more than just a random coincidence involved. There is meaning, there is purpose, there is power behind it.

Synchronicities seem like small miracles, anonymous gifts from the universe. They come as a pleasant surprise, a marvelous connection that can transform your life from one moment to the next, opening an exciting path with the possibility of growth or insight. These events are highly unlikely—and yet they happen. You're in desperate need of advice or help from someone whom you thought you couldn't contact, but who suddenly emails you or appears on your doorstep. You meet the love of your life by going somewhere spontaneously you had not planned to go. When improbabilities appear to multiply, one after another, and the usual laws of cause and effect are suspended, that is synchronicity.

PAULO COELHO

I believe this universe is whole. And so, synchronicity for me is this connection that you have, that you meet people, or that you read something that you need to read at that moment, or that you do something that is there waiting for you.

ECKHART TOLLE

For example, just running into the exact person whom you need to help you in what you are doing, to get a phone call just at the right moment. Something that coincides with what you are doing and becomes a helpful factor. And you cannot explain causally how that happened.

Think about the coincidences that have happened to you and ask yourself how they happened. Set for yourself the intention to see into the synchronicities that surround you. Do you now see other connections that you'd missed before or didn't want to see then?

PAULO COELHO

People sometimes are a little bit scared. They are scared of accepting that this opportunity is there waiting for him or her. They say, "Okay, no, no, this makes no sense," or they say, "It is dangerous, because this opportunity, this synchronicity that happened now, may change my life forever." And then you don't obey your heart, you don't obey synchronicity, you don't obey what there is put in front of you, with a label: "Follow me, listen to me, I am here." You don't do that and then you lose all the possibilities that synchronicity is giving to you.

Every time you have an improbable experience, acknowledge it as one with a deeper meaning. Remain on the alert and look for clues that might tell you more about that deeper meaning. Whenever you make out a message behind a synchronistic event, you confirm that you are connected to a higher consciousness and that you are far less likely to be hampered by feelings of fear and doubt when you align with your soul.

MICHAEL BECKWITH

As we begin to look for synchronicity, as we begin to notice that there is an interconnection of life that is everywhere, something happens. It is as if a filter drops away. And we notice that synchronicity is all around us, that this isn't an accidental universe.

The interesting thing about synchronicity is that, the more you focus on it, the more you attract it, the more often you'll experience it. And, as you repeatedly try to see the meanings and connections at the bottom of each experience, you boost your intuitive skills.

Coincidences are spiritual puns.

—G. K. CHESTERTON

Even if you don't see right away the meaning of the connections behind a synchronicity, keep asking yourself about it. The answer may present itself later that same day or week or month. And the answer may be in the form of another synchronicity—perhaps a sudden insight or unexpected encounter.

 ISABEL ALLENDE

I believe that everything is connected, that there is a certain spiderweb out there. And in this spiderweb, everything in the universe is connected. The past, the future, the universe, the planets, every form of life is connected.

Your logical mind can only show you causal connections, but at the deeper level of the soul, a large web of connections is at work. As you learn to see with your heart, beyond your personality, through your intuition, those connections still start coming into view.

 GARY ZUKAV

As you become multisensory, these kinds of experiences become more common. And as you create Authentic Power in your life, you begin to see that there is nothing random in your experience. There is nothing accidental in your world.

DEEPAK CHOPRA

You get the idea experientially when you find that you are in fact connected to the whole chain of being, the whole ecosystem, that you are part of one spirit, one consciousness.

Follow your heart. Your heart knows that you are part of an infinitely large consciousness that gives you access to an infinite number of possibilities. Your mind filters reality, but your heart sees a hidden order and bigger picture.

PAULO COELHO

From the moment that you are following your heart, your life will be full of wonders.

MARCI SHIMOFF

Synchronicities happen. Miracles happen. People show up, the exact person that you need to talk to today shows up right in front of you. Or the person that has an answer to your question calls you out of the blue. When you're living with an open heart, miracles happen and you don't have to create them from a sense of effort. They just happen effortlessly.

Synchronicity is in fact an expression of a shift in your identity, a shift from your head to your heart. Miracles become a more regular occurrence in your life. On an experiential level, you become increasingly aware of the love and wisdom of your soul. Living in synchronicity means living the life you were born to live.

 PAULO COELHO

Synchronicity is a miracle. The only thing that you can do is to be open to synchronicity and pay attention.

 DEAN SHROCK

It's a natural law of the universe: you align yourself with love and simply the universe begins to show the most miraculous ways for you.

Deepak Chopra writes in his book *Synchrodestiny* that, according to ancient wisdom, there are two signs that transformations are taking place within you that will allow you to connect with a higher consciousness. "The first symptom is that you stop worrying. Things don't bother you anymore. You become lighthearted and full of joy. The second symptom is that you encounter more and more meaningful coincidences in your life, more and more synchronicities. And this accelerates to the point where you actually experience the miraculous."

 ECKHART TOLLE

Often it is a very good sign when synchronistic events happen, helpful factors come into your life, because it usually means that whatever you are engaged in, whatever activity you are engaged in, is connected with a deeper dimension.

Once you are aligned with your soul and you are aware of the hidden order behind your everyday life, you discover remarkable patterns and opportunities. Once you are aware of the all-encompassing spiderweb of connections, even the most insignificant events are full of meaning.

 GARY ZUKAV

We all live in a universe of compassion and wisdom and it pervades everything that we do. It's there; we're aware of it, or we're not aware of it. It's there.

Tapping into Synchronicity

When we stop opposing reality, action becomes
simple, fluid, kind, and fearless.

—BYRON KATIE

Set your intention to discover what you are meant to do, now and in the long term. By asking your purpose, you open to your intuition and allow yourself to see things that your heart wants you to notice. You tap into a universal connection that will send things your way.

 ECKHART TOLLE

It is vital in any endeavor to ask yourself not so much, "What is it that I want in life?" but to ask yourself, "What is it that life wants me to do? What is it that life wants to express through me?" You can call it the totality also: "What is it that the total-

ity wants to express through me?" Or you can call it the divine dimension: "What is it that the heart really wants here?" And when you are aligned with that, that comes then as a very powerful impulse from within you—it could manifest as enthusiasm, it manifests as joyful doing, not stressful doing. In other words: you enjoy the present moment fully, you enjoy the doing. That means that you're connected to a deeper level within yourself.

The fearful parts of your personality have a particular agenda. You might feel you must stay in a job with an assured income and other benefits, even though it doesn't fulfill you. Your soul has a different agenda, and sees this job not as your ultimate destination but as a stepping-stone. If you feel stuck, do not despair or become resigned. Set your intention to stay connected with your heart. Listen to your intuition, which will help you onto the path of your dream and ultimate destination.

 ECKHART TOLLE

It is wonderfully liberating and empowering to be aligned with the heart, that which underlies all creation. And it is then that often you find helpful factors coming into your life out of nowhere. Those are synchronistic events, usually a confirmation that you are connected to that deeper level.

As you get onto the path of doing what you were born to do, you experience more and more synchronicity. Solutions will present themselves spontaneously, and usually unexpectedly, from the heart—that dimension of love, meaning, and happiness.

ISABEL ALLENDE

I think that we tap into the spiderweb of connections with laughter, with joy. Why does everything have to be so serious? Why would spiritual practice and love and everything have to have this heaviness in it? It's all about joy, it's all about light. I am never more connected to the world than when I am laughing. And I think that's the whole point. We need to be joyful.

 PAULO COELHO

It's very important to have fun. Even in the middle of something that you are doing that requires a lot of discipline, you need this fun. Fun to be alive. Life is joy. Life is to be connected with the energy of love and the energy of love has a very important component and it is fun.

It can take courage to trust your intuition and act from the heart. Even when you are called clearly to give up a secure job in order to pursue your true purpose, fortune may not exactly smile upon you at first. This may be unnerving, but remember that anxiety comes from your personality. Have faith in your heart's desire. Stay aligned with your intention to act from your heart.

 MAYA ANGELOU

I believe the heart is the only thing we can trust.

MARIANNE WILLIAMSON

Sometimes in life you don't know how to make the change. But the very fact that you are committed to making it, that you are clear that it is necessary, opens up new possibilities.

MICHAEL BECKWITH

Our spiritual growth, development, and enfoldment as a being are contingent upon learning to trust the heart and the soul.

Trusting your heart means realizing that your heart has access to a wisdom that is many times greater than your intellect. Your heart intuits what is good for you. If you really trust your heart, you will not be troubled by the voice inside your head that discourages you, worries you, or criticizes you. Cut off any questions starting with the words "but what if?" and send loving-kindness and heart energy to yourself.

ISABEL ALLENDE

If you don't trust the heart, what are you going to trust? I mean, that's all you have. When I have to make a decision, I know that the reasonable thing to do is make a list of the pros and the cons of what you should do and you shouldn't do, and what are the advantages and what are not, the disadvantages. I just close my eyes, breathe in, breathe out, and trust my intuition. The intuition is the voice of the heart that will tell me what I have to do.

Entrust every decision, whether it is life-changing or insignificant, to your heart. But be prepared to forgo instant and tangible results. You may get a quick answer to your question about what to do with your life, as I did, but you might also have to pose your question quietly several times in order to hear and understand the answer. You will receive the answer you need, if not the answer you expect. Sometimes you have to live in uncertainty for a while so the connection with your soul can take hold and mature. Hold your question in your heart, live with your question. Live the question.

> *Be patient toward all that is unsolved in your heart and try to love the questions themselves . . . Do not now seek the answers, which cannot be given you because you would not be able to live them. And the point is, to live everything. Live the questions now. Perhaps you will then gradually, without noticing it, live along some distant day into the answer.*
>
> —RAINER MARIA RILKE

 PAULO COELHO

It is because your heart is open, and because you enjoy the questions, not because you have answers to these questions. From the moment that you enjoy the questions, then you have an open door to life.

Confident that your soul will ultimately have something better in store for you than your mind can ever imagine, in time you will be able to live with that uncertainty, perhaps even enjoy it. Meanwhile, as you increase your trust in your heart, you establish more frequent contact with your soul.

Being at ease with not knowing is crucial for
answers to come to you.

—ECKHART TOLLE

 LINDA FRANCIS

You have to experiment. Try it for yourself. It's so important if
you want to change your life.

These experiments do not have to be big ones at first. You can start by trying out decisions about whether to accept an invitation or whether to change your route to work or home.

Trust what moves you most deeply.

—SAM KEEN

In following your heart, you do not necessarily have to give up your job or burn bridges. As soon as you begin to reorganize your life around your heart and soul, you sense a deeper meaning in many everyday situations. You have a renewed enthusiasm for life. Your heart is keen to seize every opportunity for growth and, as the power of your heart grows, you find it easier to place your implicit trust in the universe.

 GARY ZUKAV

Then the wise and compassionate universe becomes you and you
become a wise and compassionate expression of that.

Trusting in your heart leads to a profound peace of mind. You never really worry again, because you know that everything is taking its intended course.

 ## JOE DISPENZA

It is an interesting moment, because when we slip into this place and we feel so whole, we would never want anything and that's the moment when we make it to this place that we are at the kingdom where we can have anything. And when we finally arrive there, we no longer want it and that is when miracles begin to happen around us. And the organization of the universe begins to show up in new and unusual ways.

When you let go of fear, you are in a state of utmost connectedness and harmony with the universe. You are living your best life.

 ## PAULO COELHO

From the moment that you feel enthusiastic about everything, you know that you are following your heart.

 ## MICHAEL BECKWITH

A trust of life begins to be activated within us. We realize we're trusting the heart, we're trusting our own soul, and it never leads us wrong. The next step, we know it. We feel it. It's right there.

Joe Dispenza (opposite)

CONTEMPLATION

Everything That Happens Is a Lesson

Charlene Belitz's book *The Power of Flow* provides a number of ways to increase your experiences of synchronicities. Think of a turning point in your life or an experience that seemed like a coincidence, large or small. Ask yourself, "What did I learn from that event? What good did it bring into my life?" See everything that happens as a lesson.

Think of other experiences and turning points, good ones and bad. What did each teach you? Did any experience lead to another one? Was it good or bad? Did you seem to be directed on that path? What patterns do you see in these events? What lessons can you draw? Do you see connections now that you missed earlier? Do you see any way to act now, in the present and near future, on what you've learned?

Ask your heart how to connect with others. This will create synchronicities in your life and in others' lives. Listen for and act on any intuitive messages you receive.

If you are ready to hear it, now set your intention to discover your purpose. Ask yourself, "What does life want from me? What does my heart want me to do?"

PART 3
Heart in the World

*As human beings, our greatness lies not so much
in being able to remake the world . . . as in being
able to remake ourselves.*

—GANDHI

11. Money and Career

If you focus on success, you'll have stress. But if you pursue excellence, success will be guaranteed.

—DEEPAK CHOPRA

Money is a means of exchange, a tool to facilitate the transfer of goods and services. However, for many people it becomes a definition of success. Though undeniably important in helping to meet basic needs like food and shelter, it is an external power that cannot ultimately protect you from life's challenges or help you find your life's purpose. Money has only a limited effect on your happiness. Scientific research confirms that the influence of money on your sense of well-being is fairly limited and that an annual income over $75,000 will not make you any happier.

DEEPAK CHOPRA

We have an economic crisis, because we've built an economy that was based on a false premise. First of all, the economic crisis occurred because we were spending money that we had not earned to buy things that we did not need, to impress people that we did not like. And it was all about "me" and "mine." Our whole economic system was based on a casino mentality: all these so-called derivatives of the 2.9 trillion dollars that circulate in the world's markets, less than 2 percent was actually going to provide any kind of benefit to society. Less than 2 percent of the 2.9 trillion dollars, every day.

Your true self will never consider the accumulation of money a goal in itself, but only a by-product of something greater, a consequence of following your heart. Your heart is more concerned with having *abundance* in your life than having money—abundant fulfillment, love, and joy.

In *The Seven Spiritual Laws of Success,* Deepak Chopra writes, "There are many aspects to success; material wealth is only one component . . . Success also includes good health, energy and enthusiasm from life, fulfilling relationships, creative freedom, emotional and psychological stability, a sense of well-being and peace of mind."

 ## PAULO COELHO

What is success? Success is money and fame? No. Success is when you go to bed in the evening and say, "Oh, my joy. Oh, my God, I can sleep in peace."

*Put your heart, mind, and soul into even your
smallest acts. This is the secret of success.*

—SWAMI SIVANANDA

 ## RUEDIGER SCHACHE

*From the viewpoint of your heart or from your soul, money
is just a necessary thing for some experiences that you want to
make in your life. Your heart is not interested in money itself.
But sometimes money helps you to go on your path and that's
why money is an important thing, but not the most important.*

It is only when your actions are driven not by money but by enjoyment, fulfillment, harmony, and the desire to contribute to the greater good that they receive the support of the universe. Then you are working from your heart.

 ## GARY ZUKAV

*If you want to have more money (or if you want to have another
job) so that you can give the gifts that you were born to give,
that is not the pursuit of external power.*

*Inner values like friendship, trust, honesty, and compassion
are much more reliable than money—they always bring
happiness and strength.*

—DALAI LAMA

ECKHART TOLLE

If making money becomes your primary goal, then know that you are not connected with the deepest dimension in yourself that we call the heart. So making money as a goal is not an effective way to live. You will find, even if you achieve your goal and make a lot of money, that ultimately it leads to frustration and unhappiness. This is not to say that money is inherently not spiritual. That is not the case. It often happens that when your actions become empowered and contribute something vital to this world, then abundance in some form—and it may be in the form of money—can sometimes flow to you. Because there is such an enormous output of energy into this world through you, the world gives back to you.

When you combine personal enthusiasm with the desire to create excellence, your actions are noticed and appreciated. Reward follows spontaneously and sometimes abundantly. And because you are living your best life, there is a good chance that money will follow, too, either sooner or later, although without guarantees as to how much.

 PAULO COELHO

Your heart has a very good way to tell you whether you are on a good path or not. It's called enthusiasm. Enthusiasm comes from the Greek word that has theos *in its roots—as in theology. Enthusiasm is the manifestation of God in your heart. So from the moment that you feel enthusiastic about everything—even*

if this thing does not fit into your logical world—you know that you are following your heart. And from the moment that you are following your heart, your life will be full of wonders. And you look around and say, "My God, I am having fun."

You can only become truly accomplished at something you love. Don't make money your goal. Instead, pursue the things you love doing, and then do them so well that people can't take their eyes off you.

—MAYA ANGELOU

 PAULO COELHO

In my case, for example, when I started writing, I never thought I would make a living out of writing. I was writing because I wanted to do it, I had no choice. At the end of the day, I not only made money out of writing, but I made a lot of money out of writing. And everybody says, "If Paulo Coelho can do it, we can do it."

When you stay connected to the present moment, you have a sense of completion and abundance.

 ECKHART TOLLE

The fullness of life, Jesus called it. He was not talking about abundance of goods, abundance of stuff. Abundance on a deeper level is not about stuff. Abundance is in you inherently, one with

the heart, because it is the abundance of life itself, the creative principle itself, the creativity, the source, the aliveness within you.

You may be showered with material abundance, but you don't need it for your fulfillment. What matters most is that you do something that is close to your heart, that makes your heart beat faster. The chances are that by doing so you will feel fulfilled and rewarded and you will reap the tangible rewards.

 ## DEEPAK CHOPRA

Happiness and success are the progressive realization of worthy goals. Happiness is also the ability to love and have compassion. Happiness is a sense of connection to the creative mystery of the universe that we call God.

Sir Richard Branson, the founder of the Virgin Group, has said, "If you think 'How can I make lots of money, let's bring the accountants in, we'll work out the business plans,' it's just the wrong way around. You get one set of accountants who will say, 'Yes, you can make lots of money' and another set of accountants with exactly the same input will say, 'You will lose lots of money.' It's got to be from your heart and do something you're passionate about, which is gonna be your hobby, and it's likely to be successful."

 ## PAULO COELHO

I think that it is very important to first think "fulfill your dream" and second "money may come." And if money does not come, you

Deepak Chopra (opposite)

will still have a life full of joy, full of fun. And finally, when money comes, be responsible for that and show yourself as an example. Because life is not changed by opinions, life is changed by examples.

Fulfill your dream by listening to your heart. Remember: dreams have no deadline. Do what you can and bear in mind that when things appear to be going awry, there is a reason; the cosmic plans are much more far-reaching than you can imagine. As long as your intention truly originates in the soul, the universe will lend its full support to everything you do, and money and other forms of abundance will also come your way.

A lack of money will only bother you when you are disconnected from your soul. Restore that connection and the abundance of the universe will flow your way again. Once you are truly converted to the power of the heart, you end up shining in a unique piece of theater directed by the universe.

 ## DEEPAK CHOPRA

To get out of this mess, ask yourself, "What are my unique skills? How do I serve humanity?" Do something once in a while that is not about yourself. Do something once in a while that is not about business and you'll see that your business also improves. So you want to get out of the suffering? Build a real economy and this real economy is the economy that comes from your heart.

If you replace money with the power of the heart as your measure of success, you will be pursuing your passion and your true vocation. You will have less stress and tension, a better work-life balance, more time for your life partner, family, and friends. When you look back on your life, you will have a long list of highlights and no regrets.

 ECKHART TOLLE

And when you act out of that and you are not seeking fulfillment through your action anymore, you are simply enjoying the action. And that means it's empowered. And when that is the case, after a little while, it can easily happen that suddenly you are showered with material abundance. But you don't need that anymore.

An Economy of the Heart

People first, then money, then things.

—SUZE ORMAN

In 2006, in his speech to the Academy of Achievement, a nonprofit organization in Washington, D.C., that invites prominent people from around the world to inspire young entrepreneurs, film director Steven Spielberg said, "When you have a dream, it often doesn't come at you screaming in your face, 'This is who you are, this is who you must be for the rest of your life.' Sometimes a dream almost whispers. I've always said to my kids, 'The hardest thing to listen to, your instincts, your human personal intuition, always whispers. It never shouts. Very hard to hear. So you have to, every day of your lives, be ready to hear what whispers in your ear. It very rarely shouts. If you can listen to the whisper, if it tickles your heart, and it's something you think you want to do for the rest of your life, then that is going to be what you do for the rest of your life. And we will benefit from everything you do.'"

Everyone has a purpose in life . . . a unique gift of special talent to give others. And when we blend this unique talent with service to others, we experience the ecstasy and exultation of our own spirit, which is the ultimate goal of all goals.
—DEEPAK CHOPRA, *THE SEVEN SPIRITUAL LAWS OF SUCCESS*

 PAULO COELHO

You can find out what you're supposed to do with your life if you really listen to your heart.

Whether you are on the right track is not a question your mind can answer for you. Perhaps you have a job that others can only dream of and yet you feel that you are in the wrong place, at odds with the culture or values of your company. You simply feel that you are heading down the wrong professional path.

 GARY ZUKAV

We all ask the questions "What am I here to do? What is my mission in life?" We are looking for purpose, but purpose will find us when we open our hearts.

If this feeling and these questions are a part of your life, your heart is talking to you, trying to help you find the right road. This is why a wrong turn will often help you find the right one. When your heart speaks to you, it reveals the coordinates of the path that really suits you, a path that leads to your place in the bigger picture.

 ## HOWARD MARTIN

When you open your heart, you get access to a lot more than normal logical intelligence. You get access to things like your intuition. You get access to a new level of sensitivity and the ability to discriminate between things and see into things more clearly.

Sometimes your heart will tell you to find fulfillment outside your work environment. As a young clerk at the Swiss Patent Office, Albert Einstein had to wait until after work to pursue his true passion, physics. Only later could he do it professionally. As rational and reasonable as Einstein was, he once described common sense as "a collection of prejudices acquired by age eighteen."

Imagination is more important than knowledge, for while knowledge defines everything we know and understand, imagination points to all we might yet discover and create.

—ALBERT EINSTEIN

In *The Book of Awakening*, poet and memoirist Mark Nepo writes of his struggles as a teenager when his parents wanted him to go into professions that they had chosen for him. His mother wanted him to be a lawyer, his father an architect. But Nepo wanted—or rather needed—to be a poet, because, "something in it brought me alive."

Nepo quotes a mystic: "A fish cannot drown in water. A bird does not fall in air. Each creature God made must live in its own true nature."

Each of us must find our true element in which to live, in other words, our own true self and calling.

Part of the blessing and challenge of being human is that we must discover our own true God-given nature . . . an inner necessity. For only by living in our own element can we thrive without anxiety. And since human beings are the only life-form that can drown and still go to work, the only species that can fall from the sky and still fold laundry, it is imperative that we find that vital element that brings us alive . . . the true vitality that waits beneath all occupations for us to tap into, if we can discover what we love. If you feel energy and excitement and a sense that life is happening for the first time, you are probably near your God-given nature. Joy in what we do is not an added feature; it is a sign of deep health.

—MARK NEPO, *THE BOOK OF AWAKENING*

The universe wants you to do what you are meant to do. Everyone has a mission: to do what you excel at *and* derive pleasure from. That mission varies from person to person and can include anything from teaching children with learning disabilities or caring for the elderly to public service or heading a multinational corporation. We all have a mission we are meant to discover.

MICHAEL BECKWITH

Each of us enters into this life bearing gifts. Gifts of the soul. Gifts that only we can give, as we are unique expressions of the infinite. As we begin to listen to the heart, and not to the chatter of society, not to the noise of the world, we get to release our gifts. We get to do what we were called to do.

 ## RUEDIGER SCHACHE

Why does our purpose in life become clear when we activate or connect to our heart? It's because here, in this area of your heart, is a gateway and it's the gateway to your soul. And if you listen to what comes through that gateway, you will follow more and more the way of your soul. And if you are following the way of your soul, your purpose in life will be totally clear.

To better understand your mission, you may need to ask yourself a number of questions. The answers to those questions will lead to a better grasp of your true self.

 ## DEEPAK CHOPRA

Ask your heart any question. Who am I? What do I want? What is my purpose in life? Who are my heroes and heroines in history, in mythology, religion? What are the qualities I look for in a good friend? What are the qualities that I contribute to in a

*good relationship? What are my unique skills and talents? How
do I use those to serve humanity?*

Take a moment to answer Deepak's questions. You may want to write
down the answers, so you can go back to them later.

When you follow the route that your internal navigation system has
mapped out for you, you may find yourself taking a professional turn
that does not make rational sense, a turn that leads you down bumpy,
dark roads. Nevertheless, you know that you need to do this. Your
heart makes it clear that you have no other choice. Do not worry about
what other people think; just listen carefully to your inner voice. When
you do what you were born to do, your destiny is clear. When you do
what you were born to do, you will not feel sapped, but full of energy.

I always was a rich person because money's not related to happiness.

—PAULO COEHLO

MARIANNE WILLIAMSON

*It is coming from somewhere deep inside: the human spirit. And
it's saying, "Go that way and your heart will guide you."*

You will find out what you are doing it all for by listening to your
heart. When you are accomplishing your mission, you will know it by
the infinite pleasure it gives you.

CONTEMPLATION

Your Calling

To better understand your mission, ask yourself the following questions:

- Who am I?
- What is it I want?
- What is my true element?
- What does my heart guide me to want and to do?
- What is my life's purpose?
- Who are my heroes/heroines in history, in fiction and legend, or in religion? What is it that I admire most about them?
- What are my unique skills and talents?
- How can I use these unique skills and talents for a greater purpose?

Be brave enough to follow the route that your heart and soul map out for you, even when it seems unusual or meets with opposition from others. Bear in mind that when you follow what you were born to do, your destiny will reveal itself—even if it takes time.

To help you, you can repeat this Change Me prayer created by Tosha Silver:

Change me, Divine Beloved, into one who wakes up and remembers completely who I actually am: Everything I encounter... Let me invite your Divine plan for me and use this life for the highest good. Let me live in Divine service... Change me, Divine Beloved, into one who knows how the heck to do this!

12. The Heart of Health

The heart is the thousand-stringed instrument that can only be tuned with love.

—HAFIZ

Connecting to your heart is important for your physical, emotional, and spiritual health. Your heartbeat and emotional state are linked. When you experience negative emotions like fear, anger, or frustration, your heartbeat is agitated and irregular. When you experience positive emotions like love, happiness, or appreciation, your heartbeat is calmer and gentler.

 DEEPAK CHOPRA

In other words, your heart is structurally different in different states of consciousness. If you're living in fear, the heart structure is very different than if you're living in love, or compassion, or kindness, or equanimity.

Scientific research has shown that, when the rhythm of your heart is calm and coherent, your body is in better balance, which in turn improves your health and well-being.

 ## HOWARD MARTIN

It's obvious that the emotions associated with the heart are the ones that are healthy for us. They're the ones that regenerate. There have been a lot of studies on the effect of negative emotions like, for example, anger and things like that. They are not good for us. Studies we've done on things like care show that there's a regenerative effect created by having more of those emotions that are heart-related emotions. Care, appreciation, love, those emotions regenerate us. They are good for our health. They create hormonal changes in our body that last for a long time. The heart is having a lot of influence on the body beyond the fact that it's just pumping blood. It's influencing brain function, hormonal releases, and immune system response. All the major body systems are being influenced by the heart.

Not only is your health of crucial importance to your heart, but your heart is of crucial importance to your health. As soon as you connect with your heart and experience all the positive emotions it facilitates, you improve your health.

 ## DEAN SHROCK

Feeling loved and cared for, feeling heard and understood is actually the key to health.

MARCI SHIMOFF

There are some wonderful fringe benefits of experiencing a greater state of love. When you're feeling more love, you have better health, you live longer. On average people who are happier or who are experiencing more love live nine years longer. You are more creative, with greater brain capacity. You are more successful. You have better relationships. You're a better parent and you magnetize more love to you. So, all areas of your life are affected by your experience of living in a greater state of love.

When you are not entirely happy in your own skin, however, your health inevitably suffers the consequences. In fact, the continued stress from irritation, anger, or frustration increases the risk of developing cardiovascular diseases. Negative emotions seriously undermine your health, weaken your immune system, and make you more susceptible to illness.

 ## HOWARD MARTIN

An interesting little experiment was done here at the Institute of HeartMath one day between a boy and a dog. The dog's name was Mabel, a wonderful old sweet labrador retriever who had a relationship with Josh, the son of Rollin McCraty, director of research at HeartMath. McCraty put heart monitors on both Josh and Mabel to measure changes in their heart rhythms and to see if heart rhythms were coherent or incoherent. When he brought them together, their heart rhythms became coherent at

the same time and synchronized together. The love exchanged by living systems, by living beings, creates changes in our heart rhythms that influence how we function.

Two different hearts can actually beat as one. A coherent heartbeat is a healthy heart rhythm.

Generating positive emotions is the best method of getting rid of stress. Your heart plays a prominent role in this, because it is an inexhaustible source of positive emotions.

 DEAN SHROCK

I've found in my work that when people feel freer to be themselves, to do what really brings them the greatest peace of mind, then, in fact, it literally registers in their bodies in a way that makes them healthier. I experience that so frequently in working with cancer, specifically where people would truly now reorient their lives to what it is that was most important, and then take the personal responsibility to make sure they were doing things that brought them joy on a daily basis. Make sure also that you're paying attention to the food you're eating, what you're putting in your body, and that you're keeping your body fit.

By reestablishing communication with your heart and focusing on the intentions of your soul, you can restore a balance of mind and body and become healthier.

Dean Shrock *(opposite)*

 JOE DISPENZA

Those elevated emotions begin to generate energy in the heart. The heart begins to get a very strong signal and our field begins to expand. We become less material, we become more energetic, and we feel connected to something greater. This is the moment where we're no longer trying to control the outcome, living by those hormones of stress.

Here, Deepak talks about a simple contemplation that can help your heart.

 DEEPAK CHOPRA

"Contemplation" means that you hold the idea in your consciousness while at the same time putting attention to your heart. When you put your attention on the heart and even think these words, you contemplate on joy, on peace, on happiness, on compassion. Whether it's on peace, or harmony, or laughter, or love, or joy, or compassion, or kindness—then your heart is structurally different. It shifts.

It is worth remembering that emotions are faster and far more potent than thoughts, which means that positive emotions have a much greater impact than positive thoughts. No matter how hard you try to lift your spirits by thinking about positive things, your thoughts will ultimately be overtaken by your emotions. Positive thinking is still useful, but positive impulses from your heart will do a great deal more to improve your health.

 ## ROLLIN McCRATY

As we learn how to tap into our heart's intelligence, it increases our vitality, our resilience, and especially our health and happiness. From my perspective, people who are depressed are really cut off from what we call the heart's intelligence. Because it's really the heart intelligence that creates more positive experience and feelings in our life. So if we choose not to follow that, then the heart intelligence withdraws and that leads to depression.

When you are frightened, angry, or frustrated, your body produces less "vitality" hormone and more of the hormones associated with stress. If you have a great deal of stress in your life and you close your eyes to its causes and effects, you will find it difficult to connect with your heart, and it will be difficult to generate positive emotions that can help you get rid of stress.

But when you connect with your heart, with the power of love, heart coherence results, which alleviates stress. As a result, a hormone called DHEA is also produced in your body. This hormone helps to keep us younger. As Howard Martin notes, this vitality hormone generally is referred to as the antiaging hormone.

ECKHART TOLLE

Watch out for any signs of stress arising. It's a sign that you have lost connectedness with the heart, because as long as you're connected with the heart, there is a power, but there is no stress. There is a joy and there is an effectiveness, but no anxiety.

A loving heart in a loving body produces more DHEA (vitality hormone) and fewer stress hormones. It also produces important immune boosters that protect against infections. And, when you open your heart, you tap into positive emotions that positively influence your state of mind as well as your body.

Finally, and perhaps most important, our heart also reaches out to others. The Institute of HeartMath found that the heart has an electromagnetic field around it that is 5,000 times more powerful than the electromagnetic field around the brain. They can actually measure the field of the heart eight to ten feet away from our bodies. This field is communicating the energy of our emotions. It is both absorbing and projecting the energy of love.

 MARCI SHIMOFF

Your heart carries emotional information that people around you can feel and can sense. In fact, your heartbeat affects the heartbeats of the people around you.

You can draw nourishment from other people's love and affection, especially at moments when you struggle to generate such positive emotions yourself. As soon as you feel a connection with others, your state of mind can improve.

DEEPAK CHOPRA

The more we are feeling a sense of connection with sentient beings and life on the planet as part of the ecosystem, the healthier your heart will be. In fact, now there are studies that the number one risk factor for premature death from cardiovascular disease is hostility and resentment—what is called "cynical mistrust."

DEAN SHROCK

One of the things that fascinated me and surprised me in my work as director of Mind-Body Medicine for [cancer] centers was the realization that—while we were encouraging people to develop the will to live, they found it too selfish. They believed that everyone and everything else should come first. And so, when I wrote up my research—because my patients were living longer—I had to conclude it was not the will to live, but that it was because they felt loved and cared for. That made the difference. When I asked these patients, as I would move from center to center, "What helped you and what didn't?" what absolutely surprised me was not any specific coping skill I taught them that helped, but that they said it was because I listened, I cared, and I was sincere. Dr. James Lynch's research and Dr. Dean Ornish's research also were very clear that feel-

*ing heard and understood and loved and cared for literally led
to an improvement with heart disease.*

Co-creator Rollin McCraty tells a story of newborn twins to illustrate
our energetic connectedness with others. Shortly after their births in
1995, twin sisters were put into separate incubators, a normal pro-
cedure at the time. But one baby's heart rate was erratic and she was
agitated and crying, unable to calm down or be comforted. A nurse decided to put the twins together in the same incubator. The calmer baby
instinctively put her arm around her sister, who improved almost instantly. She stopped crying and her heartbeat and breathing stabilized.

 HOWARD MARTIN

*What brings us back to balance, what really heals us, is the
magnificent, beautiful power produced by the intelligence of
the heart. It never goes away, it's always there. Sometimes we
go away from it, but we can return to it. And when we do, it's
what can help move us beyond these feelings of sadness, depression, brokenheartedness.*

The power of the heart is love—love for yourself and love for others.
Love is the fast track to a healthy mind in a healthy body.

*Health is not only to be well,
but to use well every power we have.*

—FLORENCE NIGHTINGALE

CONTEMPLATION

Heart of Love

Put your attention on your heart and think these words: *Heart. Love. Joy. Peace. Happiness. Compassion. Loving-kindness.*

Whatever idea you hold—peace, harmony, laughter, love, joy, compassion, kindness—this idea changes the energy of your heart. This idea shifts the heart into a healthy, coherent energy and rhythmic heartbeat.

Knowing that, put your attention back on your heart and try the contemplation again. Hold the ideas of love, kindness, compassion, peace of mind, and joy in your awareness in your heart. Hold each idea as if you are planting a seed. It will blossom and it will grow into the fruit of that idea. It will nourish your heart, your emotions, and your body.

13. Love and Relationships

Love is what we are in our essence, and the more love we feel in our hearts, the more it will be brought to us.

—DEEPAK CHOPRA

The basic energy of the universe is love. The energy of love is all around you and inside you.

 DEAN SHROCK

Everything is energy. And the core essence of the universe is an energy of love or complete harmony and order. So, whenever you are experiencing love, you are literally allowing for that flow of that life-force energy. It reminds the core of you of who you are as energy. And it realigns the molecules of your body so that they function in a more harmonious way.

MARCI SHIMOFF

Love is like a radio station that's always broadcasting. Our job is just to tune in to that radio station. Imagine that you're tuning in to Love FM. When you do tune in, that is the frequency at which you will spend more and more time.

What we're missing is the truth that love is who we are, that we're actually an ocean of love. When we become more aware of that fact and we actually feel connected to that ocean of love inside, then instead of being love beggars walking around with little cups, hoping for other people to fill our cup with love, we become love philanthropists. We are just naturally overflowing in that love. It's not an effort to give it away, because we know: it's who we are.

Marci Shimoff, renowned expert on love, happiness, and success, has found in her research that there are four main stages of love. The bottom stage is called No Love, which is what we experience when we're in pain or when we feel fear, or when we're sad and disconnected from love.

A stage up from that is Love for Bad Reason, which Shimoff says is "basically No Love on painkillers." This is when we're trying to fill a void we feel inside. Usually we're doing that by using things that are not supportive or simply bad for us—bad relationship, drugs or alcohol, food—to make up for the fact that we don't feel love inside.

The next stage up is Love for Good Reason, which is when we get love in the context of a relationship or by deriving it from something outside of ourselves.

And what is the ultimate stage of Love?

MARCI SHIMOFF

*Now, there's nothing wrong with having wonderful, loving rela-
tionships, or loving the work we're doing and getting fulfillment
from that. But if we base our experience of love on that external
factor, then it can go away. It's not a solid foundation for love.
So, while Love for Good Reason is a wonderful thing, it's not
the ultimate state of love.*

> Love doesn't need reason. It speaks from the
> irrational wisdom of the heart.
>
> —DEEPAK CHOPRA, *THE PATH TO LOVE*

MARCI SHIMOFF

*The ultimate state of love is what I call Love for No Reason.
Love for No Reason is an inner state of love that doesn't depend
on a person or situation or a specific romantic partner. When
we feel that love, instead of looking outside ourselves to try to
extract love from our circumstances, we bring love to our circumstances. When you're in a state of Love for No Reason, you
feel freedom. You feel expansion. You feel peace. You feel joy. You
love just because. You don't need a reason to love.*

Shimoff quotes New Thought leader Emmet Fox about the power of
love: "There is no difficulty that enough love will not conquer . . . If
only you could love enough, you would be the happiest and most powerful being in the Universe."

Your task is not to seek for love, but merely to seek and find all the
barriers within yourself that you have built against it.

—RUMI

Like many people, Linda Francis had been looking for the "right person" for years, yet couldn't seem to make a relationship work. But her luck changed for the better when she was ready to tell herself "From now on I'm going to be the right person for myself."

 ## LINDA FRANCIS

And when I became that right person, it didn't matter whether
I had a relationship or not. I didn't care about that. What I care
about is continuing to create Authentic Power in my life.

Francis decided to stop searching for "the one" and to focus instead on her relationship with her soul. She examined her soul's desires and asked herself who she really was, what she really wanted in life, and what the universe wanted from her. She came to recognize that in her previous relationships, she had never felt good enough for the other person. Only after she had found a way to be her own person, whole in herself, did Gary Zukav, her current partner, cross her path.

 ## DEEPAK CHOPRA

If you want to have a meaningful relationship, stop looking for
the right person. I'll repeat that: if you want to have a meaning-
ful relationship, stop looking for the right person, but become
the right person.

By becoming the right person, your true self, you learn to view love in a broader perspective. You end up shifting the emphasis from an often anxious search for someone else to nourishing and sustaining your own soul.

 MARCI SHIMOFF

You start to become a friend to yourself. You become your own loving support. And that's one powerful way that you can start building a relationship on: with yourself, of trust and of love.

When you are happy in yourself, you will automatically attract the person who resonates with your peaceful, confident state of consciousness.

 JOHN GRAY

Many times, people are looking for their partner, their ideal partner, their soul mate and they say they can't find them. They're looking and they're looking and they're looking and they can't find them. Well, if your soul mate is not knocking on your door, it's because you're not ready. It's not that you're not looking hard enough. We have to prepare for that to happen in our life. And the preparation for finding the right person in your life, connecting with them, is being the right person.

A search for "the one" can sometimes become a search to fill a void. But before you can build a meaningful relationship with someone, you must be able to accept yourself. As Deepak Chopra has written, "In our imaginations we believe that love is apart from us. Actually, there is nothing but love, once we are ready to accept it. When you truly find love, you find yourself."

Lack of self-confidence can undermine your capacity to love another person as an equal. If you struggle to love and accept yourself, you are telling the universe that you are not worth the love you deserve.

> *I do not trust people who don't love themselves and yet tell me, "I love you." There is an African saying which is "Be careful when a naked person offers you a shirt."*
>
> —MAYA ANGELOU

 ## JOHN GRAY

If you want to find someone who can fully love you and know you, you have to know and love yourself. And self-love is the foundation of any relationship that works, even if that relationship is the preparation for finding a soul mate.

The first step to self-acceptance is to have the intention to give love. You can give love by helping others and by following your own heart. As you pursue your dream, you gain skills and understanding, which increase your competence and self-confidence. You show how much you've got going for you, which sooner or later will be picked up by someone whose values and goals match or complement your own.

 ## PAULO COELHO

Just try to love, and manifest it. When your heart is open, there is this energy of love that flows in, fulfills everything, and some-

John Gray (opposite)

how transmutes itself into actions. Then you see that your life is changing. And you ask yourself, "But why? I did not do anything. I did not learn a new thing." You did *learn, but not on the conscious level. It is because your heart is open.*

Embrace yourself. Choose to fully appreciate all that is good within you. Accept your imperfections and embrace the following practices:

- Create the intention to trust your heart implicitly.
- Be grateful for being the person you are. Appreciate your strengths and talents.
- Develop your skills and talents, out of which will come self-confidence and happiness. If you have a real feeling for doing or making something, pursue that, work on it, and improve it.
- Be kind to yourself. Make it a habit to articulate positive thoughts about yourself, so that everything you do is supported by the universe. Stop saying negative things about yourself.
- Do a kindness every day for someone else.
- Try not to worry too much. Worrying rarely solves problems. It just takes you away from the beauty life offers. If you are prone to worry, get physically active. Take a walk. Exercise. Do yoga. Moving your body helps clear your mind.

We just cannot worry about ourselves.

—POPE FRANCIS

- Be honest with yourself about your feelings. If you are sad, acknowledge your sadness and don't hide it. Ask your heart what it is telling you to do to deal with the sadness.
- Give yourself a break from time to time. Take the time to look after your body and to care for your soul.
- You are meant to be happy. Take pleasure in everything you do. Do not take life or yourself too seriously. Practice gratitude.

 ## DEEPAK CHOPRA

Those that we love and those that we dislike are both reflections of our own self. We fall in love with people in whom we find traits that we want. And we dislike people in whom we find traits that we deny in our own self. If you want to succeed in a relationship then look at the world as a mirror of your own self. Every situation, every circumstance, every relationship is reflecting your own state of consciousness.

The energy of your intentions will ultimately come back to you in relationships and other areas of your life. The people you meet mirror your own intentions.

 ## GARY ZUKAV

There is one sure way to attract the kind of person that you want in your life, one sure way: become like that person. If you want to attract people who are patient and caring, who will care about you,

and be patient with you, hold your best interest at heart, be available to you without strings, without second agendas, then become such a person to others, and you will attract to you people exactly like you. That's the law of attraction. Energy attracts like energy.

If you think you cannot be happy unless you have a life partner, you are likely to attract a partner who is unhappy and is keen to have a relationship with you to fill a void inside him- or herself. If, on the other hand, you are aligned with your soul, you are bound to attract someone who reflects that same state of consciousness.

 ## DEEPAK CHOPRA

You want to be attractive? Then be natural. Radiate your simple unaffected humanity. Don't be judgmental on yourself and others. Respond to gestures of love and don't put on a social mask. Just be natural. Recognize that you have weaknesses and defects and even shadows. It is not to be incomplete, it is to be complete. It is not to be flawed, it is to be full. So that is the secret really to successful relationships, to see every relationship as a mirror.

Always be yourself; resist the temptation to wear different masks. When you pretend to be anyone other than yourself, you become disconnected from your heart and from other people.

Could a greater miracle take place than for us to look through each other's eyes for an instant?

—HENRY DAVID THOREAU

Once you have found love, it remains important to communicate from the heart, with mutual trust and respect.

 ## JOHN GRAY

To communicate more from the heart, from authenticity in a relationship, we first have to set that as our goal and we have to be able to remind each other to do that. My wife is very clear about this. Bonnie will say to me, "John, I don't want to listen to you until you're talking to me from your heart." And I'll say, "No, I'm talking, I'm making sense." "No, I want to hear your feeling, I want to hear your love in the tone of your voice. And when you can find it, we can talk again."

What a simple message she gives me. She refuses to have a conversation when I'm just in my head and not in my heart. It would be a mistake for her to say something is wrong with being in my head, because that would make a very important part of me wrong. But what she'll say at times when my heart is closed, when I sound mean or focused on being right, is "Right now, I can't hear this. I need to hear a little bit more of your heart. When you're ready to talk from your heart, I'm ready to talk with you."

Always have the intention to communicate from the heart. If things have been said that were upsetting, see this friction as a challenge to start afresh, to return to your soul, and to share your feelings in a gentle way. Handled with loving-kindness, friction can help your relationship grow.

When you struggle with your partner, you are struggling with yourself.
Every fault you see in them touches a denied weakness in yourself.

—DEEPAK CHOPRA, *THE PATH TO LOVE*

 JOHN GRAY

This is growing in the wisdom of the heart, because each time you've come back to love, you grow in that wisdom. It's the key to access your inner potential to love, to connect with your soul, because your soul's purpose is to love. And every time you come back and love again, you grow in that wisdom.

 MAYA ANGELOU

Many years ago, I was married, and the marriage was touch-and-go. My husband made me very angry one day and I didn't know what to do. And so, I cursed him. When my mother came, he reported me to my mother. He said, "Mother, she used language which would embarrass me if I heard sailors use it on the waterfront." And my mother asked, "My daughter?" and he said, "Yes, she used vulgarity to me."

So she said, "I have to hear that from her." She asked me, "Did you?" I said, "Yes." Then she turned to my husband and said, "People use profanity because they don't know what words will do, and sometimes they can't find a word which will convey their meaning, so they use the thing most that has the least value, which is profanity."

"It is the ashes, that which is thrown away." So anytime you hear profanity, realize that this has been chosen by someone who

doesn't know what to say and can't find the words, and so is just throwing this away.

One way of communicating with your partner from the heart is by replacing complaints with requests. If you always complain to your partner, he or she will stop listening or become defensive. Ask yourself how you can convey your grievance in such a way that the other will understand. One way of doing this is to turn your complaint into a request. Just ask! Form the intention and make the request with love. When you make a conscious decision to communicate with your loved one from the heart, you can expect a comparable response.

 DEEPAK CHOPRA

Anytime you suffer, ask yourself one question: who am I thinking about? And you'll find you're thinking only about yourself. If you want to alleviate your suffering, stop thinking about yourself! Think about other people, and you'll see that you will stop suffering. Because when you think about other people, you establish a connection with them and you start to find that you are happier. In fact, there are many studies that now show the best way to be happy is to make somebody else happy. The best way to be successful is to make somebody else successful.

Accept the things to which fate binds you, and love the people with whom fate brings you together, but do so with all your heart.

—MARCUS AURELIUS

Spiritual Partnership

Whatever relationships you have attracted in your life at this moment are precisely the ones you need in your life at this moment. There is a hidden meaning behind all events, and this hidden meaning is serving your own evolution.

—DEEPAK CHOPRA, *THE SEVEN SPIRITUAL LAWS OF SUCCESS*

As you communicate from the heart, you create Authentic Power, exercising courage and discipline in consciously experiencing your emotions, including the negative ones. For instance, when you feel judgmental about someone, you look within and see what in yourself is triggering you to be judgmental; then, you replace it with understanding. A spiritual partner can help you with this self-reflection.

 LINDA FRANCIS

Spiritual partnership is such a different way of looking at relationships. A spiritual partnership is a partnership between equals, for the purpose of spiritual growth.

A spiritual partner is effectively a buddy who supports you in your efforts to create Authentic Power. And not just any kind of buddy, but an equal. As equals, you know that nothing or nobody in the universe is more important than you are and that nothing or nobody in the universe is less important than you are. You feel neither superior nor inferior toward others.

LINDA FRANCIS

Creating Authentic Power is the most important thing to me. In other words, my ability to change myself, rather than trying to change other people. When I find people who feel the same way, then we can create a spiritual partnership. For instance, with my partner, Gary Zukav, we have created a spiritual partnership. That means my spiritual growth is the most important to me, but I support him in his spiritual growth and he supports me in mine.

 ## GARY ZUKAV

A spiritual partner can help me to become aware of a part of my personality that I wasn't aware of and that's why spiritual partners are precious. I always know that Linda, for example, is supporting me when I become annoyed, or irritable, or angry.

Sometimes we fall in love when we see someone as perfect. Then, later, we see they aren't perfect and we consciously learn to love them even more.

> *A dream you dream alone is only a dream. A dream you dream together is a reality.*
>
> —YOKO ONO AND JOHN LENNON

Your emotional system can be divided into roughly two elements: fear and love. In every situation, it is up to you to choose between the energy of fear and the energy of love. The fear referred to here is not the emotion you experience at times when you feel physically threatened, when an animal growls at you, for example, or you are standing on the edge of a steep rock, or someone intimidates you. That is functional fear, fear that makes you more cautious. That fear disappears as soon as the danger is over. The fear that is the opposite of love is chronic fear: fear that recurs time and time again and is deep-seated.

When you align your personality with your soul, however, you can distinguish between fear and love, and can let love prevail over fear in all your day-to-day decisions.

 MARCI SHIMOFF

Meeting the Dalai Lama, I was so impressed by a particular answer he gave to a question, "How do you view people?" And he said there are two ways to look at people. I can look at the surface things about everyone that make us all different, or I can go to the deeper, more primary level and look at the things that make us all the same, the things that connect us, our basic common human essence. He said, "And no matter who I meet, I meet them and look at them with that primary vision of that essence that connects us all. It doesn't matter if I'm talking to the head of a country or a person on the street. I look to the heart and I see my heart and their heart. We're all the same."

Boy, doesn't life look different when we see that common humanity between us.

When someone makes you anxious, try to see that he or she is merely activating an anxious part of your personality, not trying to exert power over you. As you work more with that consciousness, the fearful parts of your personality will start to lose their grip on you. You tell the truth, with kindness, even when it is hard to hear.

Creating Love

As mindfulness teacher Jack Kornfield says, "With a loving heart as the background, all that we attempt, all that we encounter, will open and flow more easily. The power of loving-kindness . . . will calm your life and keep you connected to your heart."

The energy of love extends out to others—to our children, neighbors, community, even to the connections we have with people we don't know around the world.

 ## MARIANNE WILLIAMSON

Some of the greatest moments of teaching that my father ever did as a parent, he would remind us to take note. It's like the line in Death of a Salesman, *"Attention must be paid." Loving perception is a practice.*

Sending loving-kindness out to others improves health and well-being. Scientific studies suggest that practicing loving-kindness increases social connectedness, reduces pain and stress, and increases positive emotions. Also called compassion practice, loving-kindness helps you see things from another's perspective. It increases the power of the heart.

MARIANNE WILLIAMSON

There is a line in A Course in Miracles *[from the Foundation for Inner Peace] which says, "Love restores reason, and not the other way around." So living without heart might in a particular circumstance seem like the rational thing to do, or even, according to some precepts, the smart thing to do. But ultimately, the only sustainable, the only survivable option for the human race is that we begin living from heart, that we begin living with a greater emphasis, in fact, on a love-centric perspective.*

It's easy for us to talk about love, and to even be loved and to embody love as long as people are behaving in the way we behave, right? And saying exactly what we want them to say. But life challenges us to find an ever more expansive love. Love not just for my children, but for children on the other side of town and for children on the other side of the earth. A compassion that is not just for my interests, and not just compassion for people that it's easy for me to sympathize with, but also compassion for people that I might not like, and compassion even for people who might have betrayed me, or insulted me, or even worse. Love says, "feed the children." "We are the only advanced species that is systematically destroying our own habitat. What does love say? "Repair and save Earth."

Through the heart, we exercise the greatest power of the heart—the power of love.

Marianne Williamson *(opposite)*

CONTEMPLATION

Loving-kindness or Compassion Practice

Loving-kindness increases compassion. To do this contemplation, you sit quietly and repeat four phrases to yourself that express kindness, compassion, and good wishes for yourself and others. You can repeat these phrases any time—when you are practicing mindful breathing or walking, while you're stuck in traffic, when you wake up and before you go to sleep. You can also write them out on a note to put on your message board or refrigerator or in your phone. You can say these while practicing breathing, on an in-breath or out-breath, or without focusing on your breathing, whichever is easier for you. You start by expressing this love and kindness for yourself, because that opens your heart, increases the energy of love there and allows you to send it to others.

Repeat these phrases to yourself:

May I be safe, may I be happy, may I be healthy, may I live in peace.

If you have trouble feeling that you are cherishing yourself, just lay a hand gently on your heart area as you breathe in and think or say these sentences to yourself.

Now send this thought out to a person who has a positive

influence in your life: *May you be safe, may you be happy, may you be healthy, may you live in peace.*

Next send these thoughts out to a person who you have neither positive nor negative feelings for: *May you be safe, may you be happy, may you be healthy, may you live in peace.*

Now send these thoughts out to a difficult person in your life: *May you be safe, may you be happy, may you be healthy, may you live in peace.*

Finally, send these thoughts out to all beings in the world: *May you be safe, may you be happy, may you be healthy, may you live in peace.*

14. Resilience, Fear, and Setbacks

If your heart acquires strength, you will be able to remove blemishes from others without thinking evil of them.

—GANDHI

Maya Angelou's very presence conveyed vitality, energy, and charisma. A celebrated poet, memoirist, novelist, educator, actress, historian, filmmaker, and civil rights activist, Angelou wrote about the struggle to survive in a complicated world divided by racism. With myriad accomplishments, she was above all a woman with enormous compassion who always followed her heart, in adversity and prosperity, and who urged others to live from the heart.

I had the great privilege of interviewing Angelou in her home. Spontaneously, she told me why she had agreed immediately to my request for an interview: she believed that it was precisely at this stage of her full life that she could encourage others to understand why it is

177

so essential that we live from our hearts—whoever we are, wherever we come from, and whatever we have experienced.

If I had to describe Angelou in one word, based on my meeting with her, I would choose *resilience*. Angelou spoke of the brutal racism she had faced in her youth and the tragic events she had experienced and witnessed. Angelou helped civil rights leader and reformer Malcolm X found the Organization of African-American Unity, and also acted as Northern Coordinator for the Reverend Martin Luther King Jr.'s Southern Christian Leadership Conference. With the assassination of Malcolm X, followed shortly after by that of King—on April 4, her birthday—Angelou felt her world collapse.

Yet Angelou was not bitter. Through the years, she was able to turn those events into wisdom. She told me that she would not allow the unfairness of life to maneuver her into the position of a victim. All the grief that she experienced increased the resilience of her soul. "Bitterness is like cancer," she said. "It consumes you.

"You do not have to drown your sorrows, but you should always try to get the joy back," Angelou said. Then she sang the chorus of a beautiful gospel song, to emphasize her words:

> *Take your burden to the Lord and leave it there*
> *Leave it there, leave it there*
> *Take your burden to the Lord and leave it there.*
> *If you trust and never doubt, He will surely bring you out.*
> *Take your burden to the Lord and leave it there.*

Life can be hard. The course of your life will present many challenges. Setbacks are inevitable and there are forces that you cannot control: illness, a bad economy, layoffs, the death of loved ones. Your heart can help you deal with all of these and put you in touch with your soul's innate resilience.

 MAYA ANGELOU

Every day you work at it. Every day you go to the heart, every day you speak to me. Every day you try to do the right thing, by the right people, all the time.

Do all the good you can. By all the means you can. In all the ways you can. In all the places you can. At all the times you can. To all the people you can. As long as ever you can.

—JOHN WESLEY

Even if you realize that life will never be the same again, you can learn and grow from dealing with your troubles. Going through a difficult period can make you stronger. More often than not, the experience of having been severely tested and thrown back on your own resources enables a better quality of life to take shape.

No matter how hard the past, you can always begin again.

—BUDDHA

You need to find the courage to trust the wise counsel of your heart, even at moments of disappointment and sadness. Then you can begin to truly believe that a setback is not the end of the world, but can actually bring about an interesting turn in your life.

MAYA ANGELOU

That is the heart knocking on your door saying, "Open the door, here I am, you need me." Because then you say, "Oh, look at where I am, I'm in hell. I didn't know that." But the heart tells you, "Trust me, I will bring you out of that."

 MICHAEL BECKWITH

Life is full of challenges. Challenges and hardships oftentimes are the intense heat and fire that break us open to discover gifts, talents, and capacities that are lying within us.

When life does not go your way, your mind may churn out fatalistic and oppressive scenarios, noticing limitations instead of opportunities. These worst-case scenarios will make the obstacles feel like a life sentence and would have you believe that life after getting fired or the failure of your relationship is no longer worth living. But if you tear yourself away from these thoughts by entering into a dialogue with your heart, you will be rewarded with the confidence that you will eventually get through this difficult phase.

 PAULO COELHO

When you're defeated and you suffer, don't pretend that you're spiritually superior. Sit down and cry. Say, "Oh my God, why did you forsake me?" You are allowed to cry, you are allowed to be defeated, don't try to avoid suffering, this is just cheating

yourself. But give it a time frame, let's say one week, one month, whatever. And then suffer with all your strength. You know? Say, "Okay, I am going to suffer, I am going to cry, I am not going to eat, I am going to eat a lot, I am going to do this, I am going to do that, I am going to complain, I am going to insult sometimes the divine energy." But then you say to yourself, "Okay, this is part of life." Don't give up, you live this situation with a strength that you did not know you had. Don't be coward enough to avoid suffering. Suffer! That's not wrong.

I suffer a lot. I had a lot of opposition. But still, when I overcome this, and I say, "I am not going to be paralyzed by that, I'm not going to comply with what they think I should do." I feel stronger, and it is good for me.

The source of wisdom is whatever is going to happen to us today. The source of wisdom is whatever is happening to us right at this instant.

—PEMA CHÖDRÖN

 ## HOWARD MARTIN

When we make that move to go deeper in ourselves, we find the intelligence of the heart. And when we do, more hopeful, secure perspectives begin to emerge. Even our inner dialogue can change. We may end up having inner thoughts of things like "This is a terrible situation and I don't know how I'm gonna get through it, but I've been through tough things before and I've found a way. I bet I'll find a way this time." That is the intelligence of the heart speaking to you.

Because your heart has a greater perspective on your life than your brain does, it can show you a way of handling a problem. Perhaps losing your job will be the stepping-stone to a new working environment where you learn new skills. Perhaps you will find a new way to give love after losing someone you love. Stay connected with your heart and listen for its guidance.

 PAULO COELHO

All of a sudden you face tragedy and say, "Oh my God, what's the meaning of life?" And then, instead of being scared by a tragedy, you say, "I am going to change my life. I am going to do something that is important to me, not something that they told me to do."

When you can view a setback through the lens of your heart, it may not change the actual setback, but it does alter your perception of it. You can only pick up your life again when you have the courage to follow your heart and trust that your soul will take you to your destination.

 MICHAEL BECKWITH

When we become aware that challenges are a part of our unfolding of our soul, that they are a part of life, that they are a part of this incarnation, part of this spiritual quest, we approach them differently. We intend to have a spiritual practice where our focus is about growing, where our focus is about unfolding, where our focus is about becoming more ourselves.

When you can view difficulty as a test, which will only strengthen your soul, you will in time discover that, although the setback was inevitable and you did not expect or deserve it, it did help you grow.

 ## NEALE DONALD WALSCH

> *You can even be grateful for things that you imagine aren't any good for you, that you imagine that you don't really want, or that you wish you hadn't had to experience. Even in those moments, masters say, "Thank you to life, thank you to God, thank you to the divine self for this particular experience, because I know that before too long I will see the extraordinary gift that has been folded into this physical encounter."*

Setbacks offer unique opportunities to explore the resilience of your soul. You can come out of them less vulnerable and more skillful at dealing with new setbacks. You will see that the headwind you experienced along the way was key to your journey. Your survival is more precious. Love is all the sweeter. And you appreciate success for however long it lasts after a reversal.

Our greatest glory is not in never falling, but in rising every time we fall.

—CONFUCIUS

In order to free yourself from despair, anger, and self-pity, even when life is a struggle, remind yourself of everything you are grateful for. Sometimes these things may be difficult to see, but they are there. Gratitude helps you transform the scale and meaning of your setbacks and make them more bearable.

RUEDIGER SCHACHE

If you express yourself in appreciation or in gratitude, it's like sending love out to God. Gratitude is opening your heart and giving a big, big yes to God, to the universe, to your soul, or to whatever you believe in. Gratitude is one of the most powerful things you can do to open your heart.

Whatever happens in your life, have faith in a higher order, in the support of something greater, knowing that you are not alone. Bear in mind, even in times of adversity, that you are more than a body, you are a soul connected to others.

 GARY ZUKAV

A five-sensory human looks at experience as good fortune and bad fortune, positive or negative, the best of luck or the worst of luck. But a multisensory human has a more expanded perception. A multisensory human sees all experience as potential to grow spiritually. All experience.

When something hurts in life, we don't usually think of it as our path or as the source of wisdom. In fact, we think that the reason we're on the path is to get rid of this feeling . . . This is the time to open your heart, to be kind, right now in this moment. Now is the time . . . Now is the only time.
—PEMA CHÖDRÖN, *WHEN THINGS FALL APART*

Ruediger Schache *(opposite)*

The Heart Carries You Through Fear

Fear and love are opposites, but they also complement each other. Everything that is not love is fear. Love comes from the soul, whereas fear is a collective term for all negative emotions, including anger, irritation, jealousy, resentment, hatred, machismo, and a sense of superiority or inferiority or both. Fear is everything that prevents you from connecting with your heart. This kind of fear is something entirely different from the sense of physical threat you may have when hearing ominous sounds or when somebody intimidates you.

 PAULO COELHO

> *Of course there are fears that we need to have. Look before you cross the street, because otherwise you can be hit by a car. This is a positive fear. On the other hand, there are fears like "I am scared to talk to this lady or to this man, because I fear to be rejected." This is a stupid fear. So choose your fears and don't be paralyzed by the bad ones. Somehow the fear is there to test us.*

We all have fears. Of course, this is annoying, and most of us are not exactly proud of the fearful sides of our personality. And yet the moments when you feel fear provide the perfect opportunity for greater self-understanding.

> *If you try to get rid of fear and anger without knowing their meaning, they will grow stronger and return.*
>
> —DEEPAK CHOPRA, *THE THIRD JESUS*

Nothing ever goes away until it has taught us what we need to know.

—PEMA CHÖDRÖN

GARY ZUKAV

The fear-based parts of your personality are not your obstacles, they are not your enemies. They are your avenues to spiritual growth.

When somebody wrongly accuses you of something, when somebody is trying to pin something on you that you have absolutely nothing to do with, you feel victimized and angry or indignant. Still, you can determine the way you handle your anger by whether you decide to align your personality with your soul at that moment. The cause of your anger is only that fearful part of your personality, and not your soul, that views the behavior of the other person (the one you believe has wrongly accused you) as unjust. As long as you let yourself be governed by a fearful part of your personality, anger will remain in charge.

RUEDIGER SCHACHE

What happens outside is just to press a button in your system and then it activates, for example, fear or anger. And then what you can do is focus on the inner world, on the anger or on the fear.

MICHAEL BECKWITH

When we consider challenging a fear, we're actually considering shining the light of awareness on those places within us that are fearful.

Before connecting with your heart to turn your anger into love, you need to face your anger and recognize it as an impulse from a fearful part of your personality. Remind yourself that, like the person identified by your fear, you are more than just personalities but equal souls.

 ## PAULO COELHO

It is an inner battle that you have to trust your intuition, you have to trust your heart.

Place your trust in your heart to stop yourself from translating your anger into abusive words or actions. The conscious decision to turn your anger into love will enable you to steer your own course and prevent negative emotions from taking over the helm. Think of your fears as recurring gifts that give you the chance to grow.

 ## ISABEL ALLENDE

It's very hard to remember love when we are scared. Being afraid is one of the strongest emotions in the world.

It can be challenging, when you're feeling negative emotions, to remind yourself that both you and your tormentor are beautiful souls connected at a higher level of consciousness, and that your anger is no more than an impulse from a frightened part of your personality.

How do you actually do this?

LINDA FRANCIS

Even though I'm feeling pain in my heart, I open my heart. I just breathe into my heart. I open my heart and I remember things I'm so appreciative of, like my grandchildren, times when I've been at a mountain, or by a stream. I just open myself to the love that I felt before in my life. Then I can change the perspective that I've had, that this frightened part of my personality has.

RUEDIGER SCHACHE

If you're able to find in every situation in your life the bad aspects and the good aspects, then you will be able to break through all your fears and follow the guidance of your heart. Focus on the good aspects. That's your way.

GARY ZUKAV

You don't need to let these painful sensations or judgmental thoughts determine what you do or say. That is the point. They do not need to control your actions or your words, even while you are experiencing them. The more you do this, the more these parts of your personality lose their power over you. They still come, you still feel them, they still hurt, but you are no longer controlled by them.

Negative emotions will continue to arise in your path even after you've connected to your heart. If you choose not to express them, they will not govern your life, but you do need to be aware of them and examine them. You can make that choice. Open up to loving thoughts. It is only your fear that interprets another person's behavior as, say, an accusation.

Act from your Authentic Power. The other person, seen by the fearful parts of your personality as the instigator of a negative emotion, actually has nothing to do with your fear.

> When we find ourselves in a mess . . . we can make ourselves
> miserable, or we can make ourselves strong.
>
> —PEMA CHÖDRÖN

Negative emotions begin to lose their grip on you from the moment you choose to turn away from them by opening your heart, from the moment you truly love and your heart is compassionate toward others. When your personality is fully aligned with your soul, you can listen to the voice of your heart, even at moments when a negative emotion is threatening to engulf you.

 PAULO COELHO

There is nothing wrong with fear. The only thing that is wrong, is to be paralyzed by fear. I think that from the moment that you allow fear to paralyze you, then you are lost.

Every time you experience a negative emotion, you have the choice to transform it into love.

Because the intention underlying a negative emotion and behavior originates in a frightened part of your personality, the energy of that behavior will come back to you. After all, every one of your intentions is energy. And the energy you emit always comes back to you. This is the law of action and reaction, of cause and effect. So, whatever verbal abuse and anger you resort to, you will receive back from those around you. You can only break the vicious circle of negative emotions when you choose love over fear.

> *What we do accumulates; the future is the*
> *result of what we do right now.*
>
> —PEMA CHÖDRÖN

The loving energy of your soul can inspire your personality and enable it to find fulfillment in giving and receiving love.

> *Resilience is possible for you as well. Whatever your circumstances,*
> *having dignity and the practice of mindfulness and loving-kindness*
> *can transform your life into a path of understanding and love. The*
> *world needs this wisdom and love more than ever. Through our*
> *own practice each of us can add seeds of goodness to our family,*
> *our community, and the Earth. In this way, we share the true*
> *pilgrimage of the spirit wherever we are.*
>
> —JACK KORNFIELD

CONTEMPLATION

Living Fearlessly

The moments when you feel fear provide a perfect opportunity for you to open your heart and create Authentic Power. Fear is generally in your imagination, sustained by a frightened part of your personality. Trust your heart, face your fear, and recognize it as an impulse from a fearful part of your personality, not from your heart and soul. You can choose to turn your fear into love. In this contemplation, I've combined ways to address fears and change behavior from motivational teacher Rhonda Britten and meditation teacher Pema Chödrön.

To use your emotions as questions to deepen your understanding of yourself, sit quietly and name a situation in which you feel fear or anger. Think of what you are expecting to happen—what you expect you will have to do in this situation and what you expect other people will do. Are you acting a certain way because you feel you have to? Does this make you defensive or angry?

As you feel fear arise in you, notice how you are patterned to react. Stop it. Do not say what you have said before. Do not do what you have done before. Do something unfamiliar. Do anything but what you've done before.

Look at the fear as temporary. Observe the emotion or fear, see it for what it is, and allow it to leave or subside. It may be difficult for you *not* to do something, but it may be better to sit and breathe and do nothing at all. To turn these expectations into positive intentions, breathe mindfully and connect with your heart. Change those negative expectations into positive intentions. Envision how you will act from the heart and how you will extend compassion and love to others.

15. Forgiveness

The weak can never forgive. Forgiveness is the
attribute of the strong.

—GANDHI

During my interview with Isabel Allende, at her home, la Casa de Los Espiritus, in San Rafael, Marin County, outside San Francisco, she told me that she had been raised by her grandparents, as I had. Her grandmother was very spiritual and used to communicate with the souls of the deceased. It was her grandmother who had made her realize that we live in a magical world that consists of much more than what we can perceive with our five senses.

We met in her study, where she keeps a manual typewriter and where she has brought to life so many of her beautifully written books. Allende speaks passionately. Every word has impact.

When I brought up the importance of forgiveness, Allende became quiet for several minutes. Clearly this was a power that was close to her heart. She told me about the death of her daughter, Paula, in 1992, which occurred because of medical malpractice in a hospital in Madrid. Paula had porphyria, a hereditary disease but one that someone can grow old with. But the doctors did not treat her properly and she lapsed into a coma and was put on a ventilator. After the hospital took her off the ventilator, Allende took Paula home and tended to her for a year; she hoped, prayed, and begged that Paula would come out of the coma.

When Paula was clearly dying, in the hours just before her death, Allende, with her mother and daughter-in-law, washed Paula with a sponge, dressed her nicely, and combed her hair. Allende placed talismans on Paula's chest: an orange flower her grandmother had worn when she got married, a silver mirror, pictures of her niece and nephew, and a silver teaspoon. Allende saw Paula's death as a liberation for her daughter, but nonetheless felt an intense sadness and grief. She later wrote, "Silence before being born, silence after death."

After Paula's death, Allende "experienced out of necessity what it means to forgive." She was angry, but had to forgive the doctors in order to move on. She recognized that the doctors, although they were responsible for Paula's death, had not intended to harm her.

 ISABEL ALLENDE

I went through the experience of losing my daughter, because there was malpractice and negligence in a hospital. I could carry for the rest of my life the burden of anger and resentment of what happened. I could blame and sue the hospital, but I chose to write a book instead. In that book I sort of cleansed the whole thing. I understood what had happened and realized that there was no bad intention. There was ignorance, negligence, but not the purpose of harming her. I

forgave and I have been able to live for nineteen years with the spirit of my daughter happily. I don't carry that burden with me.

Forgiving does not mean understanding, defending, or approving of another person's behavior or trying to artificially suppress the feelings caused by that behavior. Nor does forgiving mean wiping the other person's behavior from your memory, pretending that the hurt, the humiliation, or the injury never happened. Forgiving means simply opening the door to your heart again and being prepared to abandon the hope, once and for all, that the past could have been different, and abandon the hope of a past without injustice.

 ## MARCI SHIMOFF

Forgiveness doesn't mean that you're condoning someone else's behavior. This is a really important point. Forgiveness merely means that you are freeing yourself up from the energy blocks that you are holding, those resentments that you are carrying.

 ## HOWARD MARTIN

Forgiveness is one of the most powerful things anybody can do. It's hard to do, it's one of the toughest things, to forgive, especially when we feel justified that we had been wronged.

Harboring feelings of resentment not only affects your relationship with the person you could forgive but also enters into all your other relationships. You run the risk of becoming isolated from your own heart. Feelings of rancor block the free flow of love and wisdom in your heart. Connect with the inexhaustible source of love inside yourself so that you can forgive and dismantle the blockages and can start living freely in love and compassion again.

ISABEL ALLENDE

It is out of forgiving that one shakes that burden that we carry along.

Forgiving means accepting that you have been wronged, but also that you simply cannot turn back the clock. While you do remember the other person's behavior, the hope that things might be different makes way for a future-oriented hope, so that you are no longer a prisoner of the past. Forgiving is not about looking back but about looking ahead. It is about realizing that there is a reason why a car's windshield is a lot bigger than the rearview mirror.

In other words: forgiving is about abandoning the notion that you have to harbor a lifelong grudge against someone. If you do, you can never really be happy. That is why forgiveness is so important. And it calls for a fundamental change in the way you view a person you could forgive. Rather than viewing that person as one who victimized you, you must view him or her as one who will help you get closer to your heart.

HOWARD MARTIN

When we don't forgive, we have judgments, resignation, things like that, that just don't benefit us. They just hurt us, they just

Howard Martin *(opposite)*

take us down. They debilitate us and they rob us of the quality of life and even of our health.

When you do not forgive, you chafe under the yoke of grudges. Rancor hits you even harder than the memory of that irreversible event from the past. Resentment is like a cup of poison you pour down your throat in the hope it will kill the other person. And while the other remains unharmed, you wind up destroying yourself.

At different times in our lives, we all have been deeply hurt, excluded, betrayed, or wronged. Even when someone specifically asks for forgiveness, it is often incredibly difficult to bring yourself to forgive that person.

 ## MARIANNE WILLIAMSON

Forgiveness is an act of self-interest. You say, "I don't want to be stuck there, I want to be able to go on with my life without this burden of the past. I forgive for myself."

 ## MICHAEL BECKWITH

Forgiveness is essential in our spiritual growth development and unfolding.

Forgiveness is first and foremost an act of liberation. You free yourself from the bitterness within yourself, from the embitterment generated by the other person's behavior.

ISABEL ALLENDE

Forgiveness is something very personal that comes from a place of love and a place where you are at peace with yourself. I think it's something that happens so intimately, so profoundly, that you cannot force it. You cannot reason with forgiveness, it is in the heart. When you reconcile with your own heart, you forgive everything.

 ## MAYA ANGELOU

Forgiveness is everything. When I think of forgiveness, I am brought to weep with gratitude that it exists.

Forgiveness is an act for yourself more than for someone else. It's for *your* spiritual well-being and physical health. It is a process aimed at unblocking all the roads to and from your heart, so that love and wisdom can once again flow freely.

You need not let the person you are forgiving back into your life. What's more, that person need not even know that you have forgiven him or her. Or perhaps they cannot know, because they have passed away. But it is never too late to forgive someone in your heart.

 ## MARCI SHIMOFF

One of the most inspiring stories about forgiveness is about a Tibetan Buddhist monk who was imprisoned by the Chinese government for twenty years. And during that time he was mistreated

very often, beaten by his guards. When he was released, he came to America and was interviewed by the Dalai Lama, who asked him, "When did you feel that you were in the most danger?" The monk said, "I was in the most danger when I thought I would lose my ability to feel compassion and forgiveness for my guards."

To Shimoff, Nelson Mandela is both a great man and a human archetype of forgiveness. Before being elected as South Africa's first black president in 1994, he spent more than twenty-seven years as a political prisoner of the white apartheid government, much of it on Robben Island, a hell on earth where guards beat and otherwise abused prisoners. Mandela's incoming mail was censored and restricted so he barely had contact with his family, but because he could not and would not live without love, Mandela chose to forgive his guards and feel love in his heart for them. He engaged them in conversation, taught them history, and taught one guard that the more you give away, the more you receive.

Because he forgave them, the guards found it difficult to mistreat Mandela, so the prison management had to keep replacing his guards. His freedom was taken from him, but he chose to be free from resentment and anger. As president, Mandela stayed in touch with several warders.

Most of us will never have to go through that kind of brutal experience, yet are we able to feel compassion and forgiveness for the smaller slights, betrayals, or discouragements that happen in our lives?

MAYA ANGELOU

When you are present, be totally present. Bring all your good to it.
Then, I think that you are allowed to see the power of forgiveness.

Once you can genuinely forgive, you will be able to let your rancorous feelings slip off your shoulders like a heavy burden, and free the love inside yourself. You will be able to breathe a sigh of relief and continue with a clean slate.

MICHAEL BECKWITH

Not only are the toxins released from their soul, they discover a dimension of their own being that is so full of light that they have never known was there before. I don't even have the words for it. Forgiveness is just a powerful way of being in the world.

Is there someone in your life right now whose behavior has kept you hostage for some time? Someone who keeps drowning out the conversation you are trying to have with your heart? Is this not the perfect moment to rid yourself of your anger and your resentment?

The suggestions below may be helpful to you.

• It is up to you to forgive someone. You can choose not to relive the pain but to go on with your life. Nobody else can choose for you, and in the end nobody will benefit more from that choice than you will.

- Be aware of the impact your anger and resentment are having on your life. Bear in mind that this impact will always be greater than the irreversible past experience.
- By forgiving, you allow yourself to be happy again and to goj on with your life. Try to nurture love and compassion for the other in your heart.
- Try to view the situation from the other person's perspective, however difficult that may be. You are not excusing the other person's behavior, but, like you, he or she is a soul on Earth.
- Take the time for forgiveness. You need not necessarily forgive someone today. Tomorrow is another day. It is never too late for forgiveness.
- Do not linger in the past, but try to shift your focus to the present moment. The past is over and you cannot turn back the clock.

CONTEMPLATION

To Make Right

This ancient forgiveness practice is a path to peace. You can use it to resolve problems or conflicts within yourself or anger at people who have hurt you.

Write or say these four phrases: "I'm sorry. Please forgive me. Thank you. I love you."

You can say these inwardly, for yourself. You can say them for someone from whom you are estranged; you can say them for someone who has died.

Sit with these four phrases in your heart. Now, feel these wishes for a person whom you need to forgive. "I forgive you. Please forgive me. Thank you. I love you."

Sit for five or ten minutes a day sending these wishes out to a person or situation. After several days, or a week or two, you will feel an inner shifting of emotion, a lightening of heavy emotions, and a lifting of your spirit.

16. A Civilization with Heart

This is my simple religion. There is no need for temples; no need for complicated philosophy. Our own brain, our own heart is our temple; the philosophy is kindness.

—DALAI LAMA

Your heart is the gateway to a higher level of consciousness, that of love and wisdom. When you follow your heart, your world revolves around giving rather than taking, and you contribute to a positive civilization.

Every act counts. Every thought and emotion counts, too. This is all the path we have.

—PEMA CHÖDRÖN

When I interviewed Eckhart Tolle, I asked how an awakening of the heart can cause transformation beyond the individual experience. He replied, "Whoever is in contact with his or her heart is connected with his or her true nature. And whoever is connected with his or her true nature is connected with the true nature of all living things. That consciousness, living in unity with the power of the heart, will create a new reality. Nothing is going to free us but we ourselves."

In effect, by re-creating ourselves and mirroring the values of our souls, our inner change creates outer change, and inner peace creates outer peace.

There was a long silence, during which I meditated on his words. For me, the circle was complete. Tolle was the last teacher I had the privilege of interviewing for the movie and this book. During this encounter, I realized, more than ever, that pleasure and joy essentially form the essence of the power of the heart, and that only the heart's power can transform our world into a new one.

> *I am only one, but still I am one. I cannot do everything, but still I can do something; I will not refuse to do something I can do.*
>
> —HELEN KELLER

> *Both the Old Testament and the New Testament talk about a new heaven and a new earth. In this context heaven is not so much a place, but it refers to the inner realm of consciousness. Your heart, you might say. The Earth is the manifestation in form, which is the reflection of the inner self. A new heaven to me is the emergence of an awakened human consciousness and a new earth is the reflection of that in the material world.*
>
> —ECKHART TOLLE, *A NEW EARTH*

PAULO COELHO

A French philosopher called Teilhard de Chardin, a Jesuit, had very strange ideas for the Church a hundred years ago, so he was sent to China. He developed a very interesting idea that there is this energy of love surrounding the planet. He says, the day that you're able to control this force, or to use this force of love like you use wind, like you use the force of water, like you use the force of the sun, from the moment that you're able to control it, to put it to use, then we are going to change the world.

In the end nations will be judged by the size of their hearts, not the size of their armies.
—ANTHONY DOUGLAS WILLIAMS

ISABEL ALLENDE

The problem with our civilization is that we have forgotten the heart, Martin Luther King Jr. said. We have separated power from love and we live in a culture of greed, of power, of violence, of possessing, and of consuming, on a planet that is limited. That is an unsustainable way of thinking and way of living.

There is a growing collective awareness that the future lies inside our hearts, and that we will be better off, both individually and collectively, if we are able to restore our connections with the heart.

JOE DISPENZA

Mind and matter are related. One of the biggest challenges that we have as human beings is really creating a bridge between the objective world, what's happening outside of us, and the subjective world, what's happening inside of us. Quantum physics tells us that the environment is an extension of our mind. So if we truly change our minds, there should be some evidence in our life. In order to create a new reality or a new destiny, we have to have a clear vision of something we want in our future—we call that intention. As we begin to find like-minded people who live from the heart and we share that same energy, we begin to bond in a field of intelligence, a quantum field beyond space and time.

Just as ions bond together electromagnetically, people who create a heart consciousness also bond. An invisible force bonds ions together and holds them together. A heart consciousness will bind us together and allow us to live in a whole different world now and in the future.

 JOE DISPENZA

The moment we move into that level of heart coherence, whether we are in meditation or in nature or Authentic Power, we start to experience a level of joy and love that is coming from within us. When we slip into this place and feel so whole, we are at the kingdom where we can have anything but no longer want it. That is when miracles begin to happen around us. And the organization of the universe begins to show up in new and unusual ways.

We, each of us, need to help create this change, this new Earth, this new universe.

DEEPAK CHOPRA

If you look at the big problems that humanity faces today—whether it's social injustice, or extreme poverty, or economic disparities, or war, or terrorism, or climate chaos—this is because we've lost connection with our soul and we've lost connection with our heart.

JANE GOODALL

If we cannot get this balance between our clever brain and love and compassion—the things that should make us really human—then the future is very bleak.

Many people in all sections of society share these worries, but we're reaching a turning point where we can get clear in our intentions to create a society from the heart.

JOE DISPENZA

You have to begin to fall in love with that future possibility to such a degree that you begin to feel what it feels like to actually live in that reality. When we begin to allow ourselves to feel this heartfelt state of gratitude or joy, the body and mind begin to believe they're in that future reality now.

MARIANNE WILLIAMSON

Ultimately, the only sustainable, the only survivable option for the human race is that we begin living from the heart, that we begin living with a greater emphasis, in fact, on a love-centric perspective.

 ## GARY ZUKAV

We are in the midst of a great and unprecedented transformation. A transformation that in the next few generations will touch everyone on this Earth. It is the awakening of a new human consciousness. It is the expansion of our perception beyond the five senses, and to meaning, and purpose, and compassion, and wisdom that are real, but not physical.

A growing number of people see that the heart is, in fact, a gateway to a higher dimension and that we are connected and receiving golden opportunities through this new order of heart consciousness.

 ## PAULO COELHO

Your heart is opening a big window of opportunities.

 ## MICHAEL BECKWITH

If you tap into your heart, you'll tap into the emerging paradigm. Your particular experience will be where you're focusing your attention. This is a very powerful time.

This new vision for humanity is a more natural, authentic way of life. It includes meaningful relationships with friends, family, and a partner. It enables us to tap into our full potential and find satisfaction in life and work as we make a greater contribution to the world around us.

 ISABEL ALLENDE

It is time for a new step in evolution. I am very hopeful, very optimistic, that it is happening.

All over the world, people and organizations are realizing that the quality of our own lives and that of the people around us improves as soon as we start to live from our hearts.

 ECKHART TOLLE

This is not to say that it's already happening to the majority of humans on the planet, but to more humans than ever before.

 JANE GOODALL

Physical evolution is a gradual process. Cultural evolution is going much quicker. Then we come to moral evolution, where we start thinking about the right way to act and the wrong way to act. And then we move toward spiritual evolution, where we truly can experience what I believe humans are capable of, which is becoming part of this great spiritual power that I feel all around us, part of nature, part of infinity, part of the universe.

MARIANNE WILLIAMSON

Many of us are seeing this in all kinds of ways in our own personal lives. And the next step is to take those principles that have trans-formed our own personal lives and use them to transform the world.

This trend can be seen in our personal lives, as well as social, economic, and political contexts. Businesses are increasingly combining their pursuit of financial profits with respect for individuals and society and also—perhaps under pressure from activist organizations—the beauty of our planet. Old strategies to maximize profit have become ineffective.

 ## MARIANNE WILLIAMSON

It is moving from fear to love. That is the great evolutionary leap, both within ourselves and within our species.

That said, choosing to live from the heart is a personal decision. Only you can choose to act from the heart.

 ## GARY ZUKAV

Becoming heart-centered is a matter of choice, responsible choice. It's a choice that only you can make for yourself. No one can make it for you.

But your decision does matter.

JANE GOODALL

The most important message I have for anyone is that every single day we make a difference. Every single day we impact the world around us and we have a choice as to what kind of difference we want to make. And if we would just spend a little bit of time thinking about the consequences of the choices we make, then I think people would start leading lives that are more meaningful.

We must not, in trying to think about how we can make a big difference, ignore the small daily differences we can make that, over time, add up to big differences that we often cannot foresee.

—MARIAN WRIGHT EDELMAN

By heeding the intelligence of your heart, you are aligning your personality with your soul, and creating Authentic Power.

DEEPAK CHOPRA

If we want to correct these problems, we have to have a change and shift in our consciousness. And the avenue to that shift is from our head to our heart.

MICHAEL BECKWITH

This is our next great leap in the evolution of humanity: a loving being that is not thinking from the small self, but is thinking

from the wider perspective of the heart. We begin to connect from our center and not just from surface personality. It's a whole different way of moving through the world. And when we begin to move through the world like this, then the realm of ever expanding good—another name for heaven—begins to be revealed on our planet.

 ## ROLLIN McCRATY

The research is telling us that not learning to follow the intelligence of the heart leads to separation, which is really the underlying problem in our families, in our communities, and, really, the larger world.

While discovering the many powers of the heart, you start living from a different consciousness. You follow your heart. You tune in to the voice of your soul. You've turned toward your purpose. Now you find the courage to do those things you feel you were born to do.

 ## GARY ZUKAV

What would that look like? That would be a world of the universal human. The universal human is a human beyond culture, beyond nation, beyond religion, beyond sex, and beyond economic status. A human whose first allegiance is to Life with a capital L, and all else second.

Rollin McCraty (opposite)

ECKHART TOLLE

And it is only out of the awakened consciousness that humans can manifest those essential qualities—the qualities that are essential to the individual human life and essential to the civilization—which are compassion, which are kindness, which are joy, and creativity, that can only flow out of that state of connectedness. And that's a new world that arises. And the new world that arises depends on, is a manifestation of, that state of consciousness. Because whatever world we create, what we experience as the world is really a reflection of our state of consciousness.

MARIANNE WILLIAMSON

When we get to the point where we have experienced this transformation within ourselves, where living from love rather than fear has transformed our own life circumstances, then we become channels. We become vessels and have the moral authority by which to state that possibility for the planet. We can state that possibility not just because it's theory, but because we have seen that transformation in our own lives.

Through the astounding power of the heart, a whole new world opens up to you, in which there is no such thing as coincidence. You transform fear into love, you accommodate setbacks and embrace them as an opportunity for spiritual growth. You forgive people who have hurt you and free yourself from resentment. All this because your heart can see the bigger picture.

 MAYA ANGELOU

The heart will be involved in everything that we are supposed to evolve into. We cannot see tomorrow's sky, but the heart sees it. We will be directed in how we should act in tomorrow's sky. More than likely we already know, but if we don't, the heart will tell us if we listen.

As you live from your heart, you will witness the effects of loving-kindness in others. The power of the heart is limitless, both literally and metaphorically.

Civility and kindness are moral imperatives.

—JANE AUSTEN

 ECKHART TOLLE

As you live from the heart and more humans begin to live from the heart, that has a ripple effect. It ripples out from where you are and then you get it back. And then it spreads out, it infects others. Your state of consciousness cannot not affect others. If you are living from the heart, then that's what you experience in others. It's almost a miracle that what you bring to the interaction with other human beings determines to a large extent what you get back from others.

 MAYA ANGELOU

The heart is important in everything we do, if we are to evolve as a species. The heart is imperative. If we are to evolve into becoming better citizens, the heart is involved in the evolution.

 MICHAEL BECKWITH

This is where we're going: heart-centered beings.

 GARY ZUKAV

My vision is a world of citizens of the universe. The universal human is calling to us, it's calling. It's calling to you.

The path is completely open. As you walk that path, you become a person of the heart. The intentions of your soul will grow a new Earth.

Every single day you make a difference. You can say, adding your voice to that of Mahatma Gandhi, "My life is my message."

THE CO-CREATORS: BIOGRAPHIES

 ## ISABEL ALLENDE

In 1982, Chilean author Isabel Allende made a worldwide name for herself with her first bestseller, *The House of the Spirits*. The book established her as a writer, and also put her on the map as a feminist force in the Latin American literary field. Her books have been translated into more than thirty languages and have sold more than 57 million copies worldwide. Her work is both entertaining and informative, as she combines intriguing tales with major historical events. Alongside her writing, Isabel Allende dedicates much of her time to human rights. After the death of her daughter, Paula, in 1992, she established the Isabel Allende Foundation in her honor, which works to protect women and children all over the world. More information about Isabel Allende can be found on her website, www.isabelallende.com.

 ## DR. MAYA ANGELOU (1928–2014)

Dr. Maya Angelou was one of the most celebrated and most influential voices of our time. Her work as a poet, novelist, memoirist, teacher, playwright, producer, actress, historian, filmmaker, and civil rights activist has been widely praised. Her body of work consists of more than thirty bestsellers, both fiction and nonfiction. She served on two presidential committees, received the Presidential Medal of Arts in 2000 and the Lincoln Medal in 2008, as well as three Grammy Awards, and has been awarded many honorary doctorates. She was nominated for a Tony award, an Emmy award, and a Pulitzer Prize. In 2011, President Obama awarded her the Presidential Medal of Freedom, the highest civilian honor in the United States. Angelou worked as a Professor of American Studies at Wake Forest University in Winston-Salem, North Carolina. Her words and actions touch our soul, nurture our body, free our mind, and heal our heart. For more information, please visit Maya Angelou's website at www.mayaangelou.com.

 ## DR. MICHAEL BERNARD BECKWITH

Dr. Michael Beckwith is a spiritual teacher and widely read author. Every week, thousands of people gather to hear him speak at the Agape International Spiritual Center in Culver City, California, a spiritual community within the New Thought movement. He has made frequent guest appearances on CNN's *Larry King Live* and on *The Oprah Winfrey Show*. Together with other peace activists and spiritual leaders, such as Arun Gandhi, the grandson of Mohandas K. Gandhi, he has a seat on various international panels. He is also one of the co-founders of the Association for Global Thought, an organization dedicated to healing the planet. His numerous books include *Inspirations of the Heart*, *A Manifesto of Peace,* and *Spiritual Liberation*, winner of the Nautilus Book Award. Beckwith has also been widely praised for his work as a humanitarian peace envoy. He is the recipient of numerous humanitarian awards, including the Africa Peace Award and the Thomas Kilgore Prophetic Witness Award. More information is available on www.agapelive.com.

 ## DR. DEEPAK CHOPRA, M.D.

Deepak Chopra is a world-famous physician, author, and speaker, with more than sixty-five books to his name, including twenty-one *New York Times* bestsellers. His work, which has been translated into more than thirty languages, has sold more than 20 million copies worldwide. He is one of the best-known and most respected leaders in the field of mind-body medicine and has transformed the way we look at physical, mental, emotional, spiritual, and social well-being. Deepak Chopra has taught at the medical faculties of both Boston University and Harvard University and has worked as chief of staff at the New England Memorial Hospital. *Time* magazine named him one of the 100 most influential people of the twentieth century. In 2010, he received both the Humanitarian

Starlite Award and the prestigious GOI Peace Award. He was the recipient of the Einstein Humanitarian Award in 2002, presented by Albert Einstein College of Medicine and in collaboration with the *American Journal of Psychotherapy*. For more information, please visit his website at www.chopra.com.

 ## PAULO COELHO

Paulo Coelho is one of the world's most widely read authors, as well as the recipient of many prestigious international awards, including the World Economic Forum Crystal Award and the French Legion of Honor. In 2007, he was appointed a United Nations Peace Messenger. In 1986, he undertook the pilgrimage to Santiago de Compostela in Spain, which marked a turning point in his life. En route he experienced a spiritual awakening, which he described in his first book, *The Pilgrimage*. The following year he wrote *The Alchemist*. Worldwide, *The Alchemist* sold more than 65 million copies, making it one of the bestselling books in history. It has been translated into no less than seventy-one languages. Altogether Paulo Coelho has sold more than 150 million books in more than 150 countries. In 1996, he established the Paulo Coelho Institute, which provides aid to children and parents with financial problems. For more information, see www.paulocoelho.com.

 ## DR. JOE DISPENZA

Dr. Joe Dispenza is a well-known neuroscientist, chiropractor, teacher, and author. He studied biochemical sciences at Rutgers University in New Brunswick, New Jersey, and graduated magna cum laude in chiropractic at Life University in Atlanta, Georgia. He is an authority in the field of neurology and neurosciences, brain function, and memory formation. He has written numerous scientific articles about the relationship between the brain and the body, establishing links between thinking and consciousness and the brain and the power of reason. He has shown that when we alter our mind, our brain changes too, and that we can reprogram the brain by breaking certain habits. Joe Dispenza is an honorary member of the National Board of Chiropractic Examiners and has received the Clinical Proficiency Citation for clinical excellence. Joe Dispenza's website can be found at www.drjoedispenza.com.

LINDA FRANCIS

Linda Francis is a spiritual teacher and author. She also worked as a nurse for three decades and is a qualified chiropractor. With her spiritual partner, Gary Zukav, another Co-creator of *The Power of the Heart*, she has written two *New York Times* bestsellers, *The Heart of the Soul: Emotional Awareness* and *The Mind of the Soul: Responsible Choice*. She is also the co-author of *Thoughts from the Heart of the Soul* and *Self-Empowerment Journal: A Companion to the Mind of the Soul*. Together, Linda Francis and Gary Zukav founded the Seat of the Soul Institute, an organization that provides educational programs and events to help people create Authentic Power. For more information about Linda Francis, take a look at www.seatofthesoul.com, the website of the Seat of the Soul Institute.

 ## DR. JANE GOODALL PhD, DBE

Dr. Jane Goodall is a world-famous British primatologist, anthropologist, and author, as well as a United Nations Messenger of Peace. She is the founder of the Jane Goodall Institute, an organization with which she has done a great deal of animal conservation and protection work. At age twenty-six, she traveled from England to Tanzania, where she entered the then little-known world of wild chimpanzees. Considered to be the world's foremost expert on chimpanzees, she may be best known for her forty-five-year study of the interaction between wild chimpanzees. Jane Goodall has received a great many awards and honors for her humanitarian and conservation work, including the Gold Medal for Conservation from the San Diego Zoological Society and the National Geographic Society Centennial Award. In 2000, the United Nations awarded her the third Gandhi-King Award for Non-Violence. In 2002, then UN secretary-general Kofi Annan appointed her a Messenger of Peace, and in 2004, she was named a Dame Commander in the Order of the British Empire. Jane Goodall continues to travel some 300 days of the year and lectures all over the world. For more information, please visit www.janegoodall.org.

JOHN GRAY, PhD

John Gray is without a doubt the world's best-known relationship expert. His groundbreaking book *Men Are from Mars, Women Are from Venus* was the bestselling book of the 1990s. He helps men and women understand, respect, and appreciate each other's differences in both personal and professional relationships. He has sold more than 50 million copies of his books in fifty different languages. His Mars-Venus series of books has fundamentally changed the way men and women look at each other's roles in a relationship. He teaches individuals and communities simple ways of improving their relationships and methods of communication. He also shows how the differences between men and women can be used to develop a healthy relationship full of love and passion. John Gray has appeared on various TV shows, including *The Oprah Winfrey Show*, *Dr. Oz*, the *Today* show, the *CBS Morning Show*, *Good Morning America*, *The Early Show*, and *The View*. He has also received a great deal of coverage in print publications including *Time, Forbes, USA Today, TV Guide,* and *People.* Visit John Gray's website at www.marsvenus.com.

 ## ROLLIN McCRATY, PhD

Rollin McCraty is vice chairman and head of the research team at the Institute of HeartMath in Boulder Creek, California, which has been carrying out scientific research into the intelligence of the heart since 1991. He is an international authority in the field of heart coherence and the effects of positive and negative emotions on human psychophysiology. In his role as chief science officer, he has carried out countless studies of the effects of emotions on heart-brain interaction and the immune system. He and his research team have been involved in various joint studies with other academic and medical institutions, including Stanford University and the Miami Heart Research Institute. Rollin McCraty has numerous scientific publications to his name, many of which have been published in leading scientific journals, including *American Journal of Cardiology*, *Stress Medicine*, and *Biological Psychology*. For more information about both Rollin McCraty and the Institute of HeartMath, visit the website www.heartmath.org.

HOWARD MARTIN

Howard Martin is vice chairman of the Institute of HeartMath in Boulder Creek, California, which has been carrying out scientific research into the intelligence of the heart since 1991. He has played a crucial role in various scientific studies of the heart's positive influence on man's health, emotional well-being, and intelligence. He is the man behind a unique scientific program that seeks to improve individual and collective achievements as well as health and a sense of well-being through the heart. Howard Martin is a much-sought-after speaker at international conferences and provides workshops for businesses and individuals around the world as well as for the U.S. army. He has given numerous interviews about the intelligence of the heart, has appeared on *Good Morning America*, and has participated in programs on Discovery Channel and CNN and in *The Boston Globe*. For more information about both Howard Martin and the Institute of HeartMath, go to www.heartmath.org.

 ## RUEDIGER SCHACHE

Ruediger Schache is a German spiritual teacher and author. After graduating in economics and psychology from the University of Munich, he swapped his job as head of the advertising department of a renowned German company for a probing spiritual quest. He was thirty-eight at the time. He spent several years in the United States and traveled extensively across various continents, where he rediscovered old traditional knowledge about personality and consciousness. Ruediger Schache's books have been published in twenty-six languages and have sold more than 2 million copies worldwide. His book *Your Magnetic Heart: 10 Secrets of Love, Attraction and Fufillment* spent no less than eighty-four weeks on the prestigious bestseller list of *Der Spiegel*, Germany's biggest and most influential weekly magazine. Alongside his work as a speaker and author, he and his wife lead the Institute for Consciousness Research in Munich, Germany. For more information on Ruediger Schache, visit www.ruedigerschache.com.

MARCI SHIMOFF, MBA

Marci Shimoff is one of the United States' greatest experts in the field of happiness, success, and unconditional love. She is the author of the bestsellers *Love for No Reason* and *Happy for No Reason*, in which she shares ground-breaking insights into the great secret behind lasting love and happiness, and co-author of the now world-famous series of books Chicken Soup for the Soul. Her books have been translated into thirty-one languages and have been featured on many bestseller lists, including those of the *New York Times*, Amazon, and the *Wall Street Journal*. She has sold a total of 14 million books worldwide. Marci Shimoff gives lectures and seminars both at home and abroad and has touched the hearts of millions around the globe with subjects such as the importance of self-esteem and self-confidence. She holds an MBA from UCLA and is the chairwoman and co-founder of the Esteem Group, with which she aims to help women get more out of their lives. Visit her website at www.happyfornoreason.com.

 ## DEAN SHROCK, PhD

Dean Shrock is a psychologist and author of the bestsellers *Doctor's Orders: Go Fishing* and *Why Love Heals*. Having carried out several scientific studies of the positive impact of joy on the life quality and life span of cancer patients, he reached the startling conclusion that the feeling of being loved and cared for has a positive influence on the life expectancy of cancer patients and that love can even have a healing effect. Dean Shrock studied at Cleveland State University in Cleveland, Ohio, and obtained his doctorate in applied psychology from the University of Akron in Ohio. He developed a research proposal for the Cleveland Clinic to investigate the effectiveness of guided imagery on cancer patients and shortly afterward began his psychological research into cancer care at the Simonton Cancer Center in Malibu, California. For more information, go to www.deanshrock.com.

ECKHART TOLLE

Eckhart Tolle is a spiritual teacher and author whose profound yet accessible teachings have helped countless people all over the world find inner peace and greater satisfaction in life. Born in Germany, he studied at the University of London and the University of Cambridge. He is the author of the *New York Times* bestseller *The Power of Now*, which has been published in thirty-three languages, and its follow-up, *A New Earth*. Both are widely regarded as two of the most influential spiritual books of our age. At the core of his teachings is the transformation of consciousness, a spiritual awakening he sees as the next step in human evolution. Eckhart Tolle is a much-sought-after speaker and teaches and travels all over the world. Many of his lectures and seminars have been published on CD and DVD. On EckhartTolleTV.com, he provides monthly lectures, leads live meditations, and answers viewers' questions. For more information, go to www.eckharttolle.com.

 ## NEALE DONALD WALSCH

Neale Donald Walsch is a contemporary spiritual teacher whose words have touched people all around the world. His book series Conversations with God has been translated into no fewer than thirty-seven languages and has changed the lives of millions of people. In addition to this series he has published a further sixteen books. His dialogue book series Conversations with God is now available around the world and has made it onto the *New York Times* bestseller list. His work has brought him from the stairways of Machu Picchu in Peru to the steps of the Shinto shrines of Japan, from the Red Square in Moscow to St. Peter's Square in the Vatican to Tiananmen Square in China. Wherever he goes, he detects a hunger among people for a new way of life in peace and harmony. He has managed to teach people a new understanding of life and of God. For more information about Neale Donald Walsch, you can visit www.nealedonaldwalsch.com.

MARIANNE WILLIAMSON

Marianne Williamson is a much-praised spiritual author and teacher and a popular guest on television shows such as *The Oprah Winfrey Show, Larry King Live, Good Morning America,* and *Charlie Rose.* Four of her ten books were *New York Times* bestsellers, including *A Return to Love,* a book widely regarded as an authoritative work within the new spirituality field. Her work is based on a New Thought approach that sees love and forgiveness as key to human interaction. In a *Newsweek* opinion poll in 2006 she was named as one of the fifty most influential baby boomers. Other well-known works by Marianne Williamson include *The Age of Miracles, Enchanted Love, Illuminata, A Course in Weight Loss, The Gift of Change,* and *The Law of Divine Compensation.* For more information, please go to her website at www.marianne.com.

 ## GARY ZUKAV

Gary Zukav is a spiritual teacher and the eloquent author of four successive *New York Times* bestsellers. He graduated from Harvard University and was a Special Forces officer in Vietnam before he wrote his first book, *The Dancing Wu Li Masters.* It won the American Book Award for Science. His second book, *The Seat of the Soul,* about the personality's alignment with the soul, appealed to millions. It wound its way into the *New York Times* bestseller list thirty-one times, where it remained a total of three years. His insight, thoughtful presence, and infectious enthusiasm have made Gary Zukav much loved by millions of television viewers. He has made thirty-six appearances on *The Oprah Winfrey Show* and has sold six million copies of his books in thirty-two languages. In 1993 he met Linda Francis, his spiritual partner and another Co-creator of *The Power of the Heart.* Together with Linda, he founded the Seat of the Soul Institute, an organization that seeks to help people create meaning, purpose, creativity, health, joy, and love. For more information about both Gary Zukav and the Seat of the Soul Institute, please see www.seatofthesoul.com.

ABOUT THE AUTHOR

BAPTIST DE PAPE

Baptist de Pape, born in 1977 in Brasschaat, Belgium, is a spiritual explorer, an author, and a filmmaker. He attended the Tilburg Law School in The Netherlands, but after graduation—and with a lucrative job offer before him—he underwent a spiritual awakening that caused him to abandon the strictly practical world of law.

De Pape explores the realm of the heart and what it means to live from that space, rather than living merely from the head. This change of emphasis led directly to some astonishingly synchronistic events.

From his spiritual awakening blossomed the concept of a movie in which he would interview the leading spiritual teachers, authors, and scientists of today. Baptist went on to film and become good friends with many of his interviewees and was generously helped by Gary Zukav, Eckhart Tolle, Maya Angelou, Isabel Allende, and others. For more on the book and film, please visit www.thepoweroftheheart.com.

🖑 www.thepoweroftheheart.com
🅵 The Power of the Heart
🐦 #TPOTH

SIMON GREINER

Simon Greiner is a designer and illustrator from Sydney who lives in Brooklyn, New York. His work has been featured in *Grantland* and on the front cover of the *New Yorker*. Greiner has illustrated and authored several books.

ACKNOWLEDGMENTS

From the bottom of my heart I would like to acknowledge and express my gratitude to the eighteen Co-creators of *The Power of the Heart*: Isabel Allende, Maya Angelou, Michael Beckwith, Deepak Chopra, Paulo Coelho, Joe Dispenza, Linda Francis, Jane Goodall, John Gray, Rollin McCraty, Howard Martin, Ruediger Schache, Marci Shimoff, Dean Shrock, Eckhart Tolle, Neale Donald Walsch, Marianne Williamson, and Gary Zukav. Through their insights and inspiring stories, they have made unique contributions to my own vision and journey.

The Power of the Heart is a project that I have completed together with two very precious friends: Arnoud Fioole and Mattijs van Moorsel. I wish to thank both of them for joining me in this wonderful adventure. Without them, this project would never have become reality. Special thanks to Arnoud for joining me in writing this book.

I also wish to thank my dear friends Steven Goldhar, Allan Hunter, Evelien Peelen, Ivo Valkenburg, Gary Zukav, Linda Francis, and Marci Shimoff for their unlimited love and support.

Thank you also to the following people:

Judith Curr, the driving force behind Simon & Schuster's Atria Books, and her magnificent team, including her excellent editor Leslie Meredith. And, of course, the team of VBK/Kosmos in The Netherlands: Wiet de Bruijn, Martine Litjens, Dorien van Londen, Pieter de Boer, Simone Regouin, and Yolande Michon.

Alain de Levita and his dedicated team of NL Film, and Drew Heriot, the director of the movie *The Power of the Heart*.

A couple of special supporters of our project: Annemarie Fioole-Bruining, Rietje van Moorsel, Fleur van Dijk, Carolyn Rangel, Kim Eng, Wendy Zahler, Simon Greiner, Frans Schraven, Han Kooreneef, Richard Rietveld, Ted Baijings, Fred Matser, Aldo de Pape, Bob Levine, Lilou Mace, Gaby Boehmer, Kim Forcina, and Len Branson.

And finally, my dear parents, Thera Lubbe Bakker and Arnold de Pape.

Text by Baptist de Pape and Arnoud Fioole • Contributions by Isabel Allende; Maya Angelou; Michael Beckwith; Deepak Chopra; Paulo Coelho; Joe Dispenza; Linda Francis; Jane Goodall; John Gray; Rollin McCraty; Howard Martin; Ruediger Schache; Marci Shimoff; Dean Shrock; Eckhart Tolle; Neale Donald Walsch; Marianne Williamson; and Gary Zukav • Illustrations and design by Simon Greiner, Inc. • Interior paging by Dana Sloan • Art director Jeanne Lee • President and publisher Judith Curr • Editor Leslie Meredith • Production editor Jessica Chin • Film producers Baptist de Pape, Arnoud Fioole, and Mattijs van Moorsel • Film director Drew Heriot

PHOTO CREDITS

Page ii: Photo copyright Balazs Kovacs Images / Shutterstock; Page viii: Portrait of Baptist de Pape by Gerry Hurkmans; Page 8: Getty Images by Betsie Van Der Meer; Page 14: Photo copyright melis / Shutterstock; Page 22: Photo copyright MJTH / Shutterstock; Page 24: Portrait of Neale Donald Walsch by Christopher Briscoe; Page 27: Portrait of Marci Shimoff by Kate sZatmari; Page 32: Brand New Images / Getty Images; Page 35: Portrait of Paulo Coelho by Paul Macleod; Page 44: Photo copyright XiXinXing / Shutterstock; Page 49: Portrait of Jane Goodall by Stuart Clarke; Page 53: Portrait of Michael Beckwith by Rawtographer; Page 58: Tim Robberts / Getty Images; Page 66: Photo copyright Subbotina Anna / Shutterstock; Page 69: Portrait of Eckhart Tolle by David Ellingsen; Page 78: Photo copyright MJTH / Shutterstock; Page 83: Portrait of Linda Francis by Christopher Briscoe; Page 86: Portrait of Gary Zukav by Christopher Briscoe; Page 92: Photo copyright Kichigin / Shutterstock; Page 95: Portrait of Maya Angelou by Perry Hagopian / Contour by Getty Images; Page 105: Portrait of Isabel Allende by Lori Barra; Page 108: Photo copyright Eugene Sergeev / Shutterstock; Page 122: Portrait of Joe Dispenza by Stacey McRae Photography; Page 126: RunPhoto / Getty Images; Page 133: Portrait of Deepak Chopra by Todd MacMillan @ gotoddrun; Page 142: Photo copyright Surkov Vladimir / Shutterstock; Page 147: Portrait of Dean Shrock © Chris Graamans; Page 154: Photo copyright Rock and Wasp / Shutterstock; Page 161: Portrait of John Gray courtesy of the author; Page 172: Portrait of Marianne Williamson by Rich Cooper; Page 176: Nicholas Monu / Getty Images; Page 185: Portrait of Ruediger Schache by Christoph Vohler; Page 194: Photo copyright MJTH / Shutterstock; Page 199: Portrait of Howard Martin by Gabriella Boehmer—Heartmath Public Relations; Page 206: Photo copyright Balazs Kovacs Images / Shutterstock; Page 216: Portrait of Rollin McCraty by Gabriella Boehmer—Heartmath Public Relations.